MAYBE I'M THE PROBLEM: HEALING THE MAN IN THE MIRROR

A Practical Guide to Overcoming Self-Sabotage

NAPOLEON BRADFORD

Printed in the United States of America

First Edition, 2025

HARDBACK ISBN: 979-8-218-81468-7

PAPERBACK ISBN: 979-8-218-81469-4

EBOOK ISBN: 979-8-3507-0934-6

Red Pen Edits and Consulting, LLC

www.redpeneditsllc.com

TABLE OF CONTENTS

Foreword   **1**

Acknowledgements   **3**

Introduction   **5**

**SECTION ONE: WHEN THE MIRROR BREAKS –
NAMING THE WOUND**   **19**

Chapter 1   **21**

When The Man In The Mirror Is A Mess   *21*

Chapter 2   **33**

The Blueprint Was Broken   *33*

Chapter 3   **45**

The Brother's BaseMENt – Silent Scars, Shared Struggles   *45*

SECTION ONE SUMMARY: NAMING THE WOUND 59

**SECTION TWO: FROM WOUNDS TO WISDOM –
HEALING THE MAN WITHIN**   **61**

Chapter 4   **63**

Sabotage Scripts – When the Lies Sound Like Truth   *63*

Chapter 5   77

Unlearning Survival – The Cost of Hustling While Hurting   *77*

Chapter 6   95

I'm Working on Me – Breaking the Habit of Hurting Myself   *95*

Chapter 7   109

Messy Maturity, Coming to Yourself in the Pigpen   *109*

SECTION TWO SUMMARY: FROM WOUNDS TO WISDOM, HEALING THE MAN WITHIN   119

SECTION THREE: WHO I REALLY AM, RECLAIMING AND REFORMING THE TRUTH OF MY IDENTITY   121

Chapter 8   125

Relearning and Remembering Who I Am, Context from Creation   *125*

Chapter 9   145

Fixing Flawed Formation,
Taking Off What No Longer Serves You   *145*

Chapter 10   161

I Know Who I Am, Standing in the Power of Your Identity   *161*

Chapter 11   177

More Than Meets the Eye, Living Beyond What They See   *177*

Chapter 12   189

Made More Than Enough, Resting in God's Design   *189*

Chapter 13   201

I Am Who God Says I Am, Standing in Your Assignment   *201*

Chapter 14   223

I Have Nothing to Prove, Standing Firm in Who God Says I Am 223

Epilogue   241

Keep Looking in the Mirror, Until You Don't See the Problem Anymore   *241*

Napoleon's Epilogue   245

The Man in the Mirror, Today   *245*

About The Author   249

FOREWORD

By **Karen Hilton Bradford, Ed.D.**

Friend, Wife, Ministry Partner & Transformational Companion

Napoleon and I first met over 40 years ago in Mrs. Earnhardt's first-grade classroom. At the time, I could never have imagined dating, let alone marrying him. And yet, here we are, standing at the threshold of our silver anniversary, celebrating 25 years of marriage, ministry, and mutual transformation. What began as a childhood friendship has evolved into a covenantal partnership grounded in faith, forged by fire, and fueled by a shared purpose.

According to Verywell Mind, self-sabotage often becomes a coping mechanism, a way to survive trauma rather than confront it. For Black men especially, early experiences of abandonment, shame, or emotional silence can plant seeds of distrust that choke future relationships. When our earliest attachments are shaped by inconsistency or neglect, the soul learns to expect failure, even from the good.

This book, *Maybe I'm the Problem*, is not a clinical analysis wrapped in theory. It is a theologically rooted, soul-centered offering that transforms personal wounds into sacred wisdom. It is a narrative of lived experience; marked by critical reflection, spiritual insight, and solution-focused strategies. This book does not demand perfection; it invites you to experience "micro-wins" that multiply into lasting healing. These victories are not just emotional; they are spiritual, echoing the biblical pattern of resurrection: what has been broken can rise again.

After completing his first doctoral project with a national cohort of Black men, Napoleon uncovered more than data; he discovered

1

brothers. That study became the wind beneath his wings, marking a healing turning point in his own sense of worth and identity. In his second doctoral journey, he began to excavate the role of the Black Church in either reinforcing or resisting cycles of self-sabotage. What emerged was not just scholarship, but a clear calling; to interrupt harm and reimagine help.

As a pastor, counselor, and military chaplain, Napoleon embodies the ministry of healing from pulpit to base, from altar to therapy room. His work is a goldmine for anyone seeking liberation from destructive cycles, especially Black men longing to become the healed, whole, and holy versions of themselves.

This book offers more than insight; it offers an invitation. Through clear language, practical tools, and spiritual resonance, Napoleon gradually releases responsibility from himself to you, the reader. He doesn't just write about accountability; he models it. He gives you the courage to face the mirror, not to shame yourself, but to see yourself rightly, as God sees you.

If you're willing to embrace transformation, *Maybe I'm the Problem* can be your turning point. Like the snake shedding its skin, this book invites you to let go of what no longer serves your wholeness. Healing is not an event, it is a practice. And this book is your guide.

I've witnessed that healing firsthand; in Napoleon, in our son, Napoleon Koren, and in the thousands who this work has impacted. As you read, I pray you'll find the courage to heal, the strength to transform, and the freedom to become.

You were not created to sabotage your own story. You were created to live it well; with God, in truth, and on purpose.

ACKNOWLEDGEMENTS

I thank GOD for GOD's Grace.

I thank my parents,

Napoleon Franklin and Ella Rose Bradford,

for birthing and rearing me.

I thank my siblings for putting up with me.

I thank Karen for her mercy and for living and believing in our vows.

I thank my children and grandchildren for loving me and giving me a reason to be better in order to reimagine my legacy.

Finally, I thank Dr. Jeanine Williams, my writing coach, for pushing me and not allowing me to not bring out the best in me in order to impact my reader.

Let's journey to healing together!

INTRODUCTION

Before the lights, before the Facebook and Instagram pages, before the TikTok, before the degrees, before the pulpit and the sermons – there was a boy. That boy was me. I grew up in the church. I memorized Scriptures. I shouted at revivals. I accepted Christ at the age of seven and was baptized in December 1984. I was told I was chosen, favored, and set apart. I was raised by two devout, God-fearing parents, deeply involved in church life, youth ministry, and eventually even worked at the church. But underneath my Sunday suit, I was already broken in ways I didn't have words for.

No one ever explained that it's possible to know religion without truly knowing yourself. I didn't realize I could serve God and still doubt that I was worthy of His love. Church was a place I learned how to perform, but not how to process. I learned how to say, "Yes, LORD" while silently asking, "Who am I really?" I was affirmed for my gifts, but not formed in my identity. What I knew about ministry was public, but what I lacked in personal healing was private. My spiritual development and emotional maturity were out of sync. And that disconnection would eventually cost me.

The church taught me how to worship, but the world taught me how to desire. My ideas about manhood and sex weren't shaped by Scripture, they were shaped by exposure: my father's photo albums, adult magazines in my uncle's closet, and conversations with older peers. The church gave me responsibilities, but the world fed my appetite.

Even though I could quote Scripture and preach sermons, I was silently drowning. I looked strong in public, but privately, I was unraveling. I kept smiling on Sundays while spiraling during the week. Sex became a coping mechanism. I started to believe that my value came from what I could achieve or conquer, not from who God said I was.

I learned manhood not from the Scriptures, but from the shadows. The world discipled me long before the Word did. Sex became a language I didn't know how to stop speaking. Lust became my default setting. I believed that as long as I could preach with power, I didn't have to confront my pain.

Collision Course

By high school, I was already carrying the shame of STDs, secrets, and soul ties. I chased older women for validation and was sneaking out, breaking house rules that my parents tried to hold up as sacred. I learned how to compartmentalize. I could cry during worship and still lie after service. I could raise my hands in praise, and use them for sin in the same night.

In college, the pattern intensified, multiple relationships, pregnancies, betrayals, and deep emotional wounds. I saw pain on the faces of women I never meant to hurt. I made promises I couldn't keep. And still, I thought I was called. Because I was smart. Because I had a gift. Because people clapped.

Even marriage didn't stop the cycle. I couldn't stop. I carried every unhealed wound into my covenant. I said, "I do," but I didn't know how to be present, faithful, or honest. I wanted to change, but I didn't know how. I didn't know what wholeness looked like. I didn't cheat because I lacked love, I cheated because I lacked identity. Because I didn't believe wholeness was possible. Because I had never seen it modeled.

Work and school didn't stop the cycle either. If anything, they gave me more ways to hide. More reasons to perform. More access to cover the truth. Even full-time ministry didn't help. It only got worse, until everything collapsed.

The Implosion

On January 25, 2017, 39 days after the death of our 12-year-old daughter, Noelle Kannise, in a horrific car accident and on the day of Karen and my 16th wedding anniversary, Karen received in the mail at work and at home, two letters from two different women describing in details my sexual infidelity with them. These letters were strategically sent to Karen while I was away at an intensive for Seminary with hopes that by the time I returned Karen would have packed her bags and left me. Letters were also sent to my church, my pastor, the Chairmen of the Deacon board and to several key leaders at the church. Not only did the letters address their involvement with me, but suggested they were a representative sample of several women in Sumter that had had intimate and inappropriate relationships with me. These letters not only exposed my own indiscretions and adultery, they had lasting impact on my ministry, my marriage, and my family. I was messed up, sick, and toxic, I needed help, but I never thought that the impact would be so scandalous.

The scandal wasn't a surprise, it was the logical outcome of unchecked wounds. I really thought I was invincible, until I was exposed. Eventually, everything came crashing down, and when it did, it was loud. Painful. Public. A public scandal exposed the double life I had been leading. My family suffered. My ministry was shaken. My soul was in ruins.

I lost credibility. I lost connections. I almost lost my mind. I disappointed people I loved. I embarrassed people I led. And for a while, I thought I had also lost my marriage and my GOD. But the truth is, the exposure didn't destroy me, it delivered me. That moment of public exposure became the beginning of my private healing.

For the first time, I had to face the man in the mirror. No performance. No pulpit. Just the brokenness I had been masking with charisma. That mirror moment didn't feel holy, but it was. Because it was the moment I finally told the truth.

And telling the truth made room for grace.

Therapy, Tears, and Truth

I didn't find healing in a revival service. I found it in a counselor's office. I found it in honest conversations with brothers who weren't afraid of my mess. I found it in Scriptures I had once used as weapons, but now needed as a lifeline.

Therapy helped me trace the lies I believed back to the wounds that birthed them. It helped me stop asking, "What's wrong with me?" and start asking, "What happened to me?" With the help of a clinical therapist, I began examining the roots of my pain. I discovered that my formation had been flawed. How masculinity had been handed to me through the lens of conquest, not covenant. How ministry had praised my performance but ignored my pathology. How I had inherited silence as a strategy and shame as a spiritual gift. I had been celebrated for what I could do, but not healed from what I had endured. I had been surrounded by people who applauded my gifts but ignored my emotional wounds. I was shaped by silence, secrecy, and shame.

But slowly, I started to heal. I started to believe that wholeness was possible. I started to see myself as more than a cautionary tale.

I started to rebuild.

I was able to eventually find a healing place with a fellowship founded by one of my professors at the Samuel DeWitt Proctor School of Theology at Virginia Union University. Three years prior to my exposure, I was introduced to Bishop John Eric Guns in a class called Transformative Preaching. During the class, he shared some of his struggles, and he became a mentor and pastor-figure for me. He introduced me to a fellowship, that I initially joined to be exposed to other pastors and to be closely aligned with him, but I found so much more. At Kingdom Fellowship International, a safe place for pastors founded by Bishop John E. Guns, I found other pastors who were silently suffering, men struggling with addiction, divorce, burnout, and depression. Like me, their identities had been formed by false narratives, not biblical truth. We didn't need more preaching. We needed permission to heal. We needed a new understanding of what it meant to be whole men of faith.

A Word to My Brothers

This book is not just about my journey. It's about all of us, men who are tired of pretending and ready to heal. It's about every man who's ever been praised for his talent but ignored in his trauma. It's for the pastors who preach about freedom but live in quiet bondage. It's for the sons who never heard "I'm proud of you" without a condition attached. It's for the husbands trying to love while limping. It's for the brothers who've learned to smile on stage while crying in secret.

This book is for the men, Black Men in particular, for that is who I am. This book is for the pastors, Black Pastors who pastor Black Churches, and have the responsibility of integriously leading their people to healing and wholeness, for that is my context.. The leaders, the husbands, and the sons who are asking deeper questions about who they are and who God called them to be. And while other audiences may resonate with this and become better by this, the aim is to help those who look like me and live like me to be better.

Brothers, I want to tell you something I wish someone had told me a long time ago:

You don't have to keep sabotaging your calling to survive your wounds. You don't have to keep bleeding in silence. You don't have to keep performing to prove you matter. You don't have to keep using your gift as a cover-up for your grief.

You are not too broken to be made whole.

This isn't a book for perfect people. It's for honest ones.

If the reflection in your mirror makes you cringe, you're not alone. If you've ever sabotaged your own growth or doubted your ability to recover, this book is for you.

Let's stop hiding. Let's start healing. Let's rediscover the man GOD intended.

This is where my healing began, and where yours just might begin too.

This book is part confession, part roadmap, and part revolution.

It's not a quick fix.

It's not a manual for perfection.

It's not a self-help pep talk to make you feel better for a day.

This book is a survival guide for the gifted, for men who are celebrated in public but suffocating in private.

It's a grace-soaked letter to the broken, to every man who knows what it feels like to succeed outwardly while silently sabotaging himself.

It's a mirror, held up to your soul, so you can finally see who God says you are beneath the masks, the medals, and the mess.

We'll talk about:

- How your identity was formed, and how it can be healed and reformed

- Why we sabotage our own success, and how to stop

- The power of naming your wounds and rewriting the script of your story

- How to find real brotherhood and accountability that doesn't shame you but strengthens you

- What manhood looks like when it's shaped by God's hands, not cultural lies

- How to move from hustling for approval to walking in wholeness

And we're going to do it in plain language, with honesty, theology, story, and hope.

You don't have to be a preacher to read this.

You don't have to be perfect to start this.

You don't even have to believe you can change yet, you just have to be tired of pretending.

This book is an invitation:

to stop hiding,

to start healing,

and to finally see yourself the way God has always seen you, whole, healed, and enough.

Words to Remember

These terms will appear often in this book. They're more than definitions, they're keys to understanding your story and God's healing process.

Biblically-Based

Definition: Rooted in the truth of Scripture.

Why It Matters: Culture changes, but GOD's Word doesn't.

Example: A biblically-based teaching reminded me that GOD's mercy renews every morning, even after failure.

Reflection: What has GOD's Word revealed about your identity?

_____

_____

_____

_____

_____

Biblically-Based Identity

Definition: Understanding who you are through the lens of Scripture.

Why It Matters: Your true identity isn't defined by your past, it's defined by your CREATOR.

Example: Romans 8:1 reminded me that I'm not condemned. That truth changed everything.

Reflection: Are you living by GOD's truth or by someone else's expectations?

_____

_____

_____

_____

_____

Identity Formation

Definition: The process of developing your sense of self through family, culture, faith, and personal experiences.

Why It Matters: Formation determines direction.

Example: I learned distorted views of manhood through silence, not Scripture.

Reflection: Who or what shaped your definition of manhood?

_____

_____

_____

_____

_____

Self-Efficacy

Definition: The belief in your ability to succeed or overcome challenges.

Why It Matters: You can't move forward if you don't believe you can.

Example: Therapy showed me that even small steps build confidence.

Reflection: Where in your life do you doubt your strength?

_____

_____

_____

_____

_____

Self-Identity

Definition: How you define and see yourself.

Why It Matters: If you don't define yourself, someone else will.

Example: I thought I was only valuable if I performed. But GOD valued me because I existed.

Reflection: Who are you when no one is watching?

_____

_____

_____

_____

_____

Self-Inflicted Wounds

Definition: The pain we cause ourselves through our decisions.

Why It Matters: Healing starts with honesty.

Example: My choices caused pain to others and to myself, but naming the truth began the healing.

Reflection: What wounds are you still carrying that you caused?

_____

_____

_____

_____

_____

Self-Sabotage

Definition: Behaviors that prevent your progress or healing.

Why It Matters: You can't walk in purpose while staying in patterns.

14

Example: I turned down opportunities because I believed I didn't deserve them.

Reflection: What behavior keeps getting in the way of your growth?

_____

_____

_____

_____

_____

Reflection Questions

- Who were the loudest voices in your formation – and what did they teach you about being a man?

  _____

  _____

  _____

  _____

  _____

- What kind of manhood were you taught, and how has that affected your identity?

  _____

  _____

  _____

  _____

  _____

- In what ways have silence and secrecy distorted your self-worth?

  _____

  _____

  _____

  _____

  _____

- Who encouraged your gifts but ignored your emotional needs?

_____

_____

_____

_____

_____

- What have you been afraid to confess, even to yourself?

_____

_____

_____

_____

_____

- What are the risks of continuing to pretend you're okay?

_____

_____

_____

_____

_____

- If God could change one part of your heart today, what would you ask Him to heal?

_____

_____

_____

_____

_____

> *Scripture Meditation*
> *Psalm 34:18*
> *"The Lord is close to the brokenhearted and saves those who are crushed in spirit."*

Prayer:

"GOD, I'm tired of pretending. I'm tired of performing. Show me who I am beyond the pain, beyond the past, beyond the public. Help me heal. Help me rebuild. And walk with me as I rediscover the man YOU always intended me to be. Amen."

SECTION ONE

WHEN THE MIRROR BREAKS – NAMING THE WOUND

Before you can heal what's broken, you have to see it. You have to name it. You have to stop pretending that performance equals peace.

This section is the mirror.

Section One exposes the deep fractures that many men, especially Black male leaders, carry silently. It begins with the brutal honesty of reflection: not what others see, but what we've been afraid to admit. From there, we dismantle the lies we were taught to live by: blueprints drawn in silence, wounds ignored behind pulpits, and patterns of sabotage inherited like secondhand clothes.

These chapters are not here to condemn you. They're here to confront the cycle. They are about truth-telling, soul-searching, and beginning again.

In these pages, we rediscover that God doesn't just anoint the gifted, He heals the grieving. He doesn't call the perfect, He reforms the willing.

Section One is not the whole story. But it is the beginning of your becoming.

CHAPTER 1

WHEN THE MAN IN THE MIRROR IS A MESS

There are moments in life when mirrors don't lie. They don't flatter, hide, or protect. They reflect. Raw, unfiltered, honest. That's what happened to me. There came a moment when I looked in the mirror and saw not the preacher, not the husband, not the leader, but the mess. I didn't flinch. I froze. Because for the first time, I was truly seeing myself.

I knew what I thought I looked like. I knew the look I was trying to project: confident, composed, in control. I had the wardrobe, the cologne, the clean shave. But underneath the polish was panic. I was emotionally hemorrhaging, but I had mastered the art of cosmetic spirituality.

That moment came after a Sunday where the pulpit was fire, the people were shouting, and the offering was generous. But back in my hotel bathroom, stripped of audience and armor, I caught my reflection. And the mirror didn't lie.

This chapter will allow us to look beyond the facade of fancy suits, cologne, and shoes that are often used to mask and cover-up the corrosion and corruption underneath. This is the chapter that deals with the un-made up man and the naked truth that this man holds to help begin their healing.

The Church Clothes We Wear

I've always been good at showing up. At wearing the uniform of success. I knew how to say "Yes, Lord" at the altar and "I'm good" in the hallway. I was a church kid through and through, baptized early, quoted Scripture fluently, started working in ministry as a teenager.

But let me tell you something I wish someone had told me earlier: **You can be in church your whole life and still be lost inside.**

The church gave me a pulpit, but it didn't fix what was broken in my formation. I didn't know that the deeper issues, my identity, my view of manhood, my beliefs about love and worth, were being shaped not by God's Word, but by my wounds and the world around me.

I was formed in confusion. And I wore it like a custom-fit suit. On the outside, I looked like a rising star in the church. On the inside, I was unraveling.

A Defining Fall

It wasn't during a church service. It wasn't at an altar. It was in my bathroom on December 21, 2016, the night before I was to preach the Eulogy for my daughter, Noelle Kannise. My Bible study group called "Word and Wings" had invited me out for our normal gathering at Applebees, but what I didn't know was that the two women I had sexual relationships with would not only be there, for they had been before, but would have figured out about each other. These women had both been at the "setting up" at our house earlier, and one had left her car there. She asked me to take her back to her car, and we had an argument when she informed me she knew about the other. She became violent in the car, striking me in the face a few times, disgustedly releasing her frustration as I maneuvered the car home, and once she left and I got inside, I collapsed feeling disgusted with myself. With a bag of ice on my face to attempt to minimize the swelling, I stood looking at the man in the mirror.

My face was puffy from crying. My hands were trembling. My soul felt corroded. And in that quiet space between another lie and a sermon, GOD let me see what I had become.

It wasn't the fall that hurt the most, it was the realization that I'd accepted this double life as normal. That I had come to believe pain was the price of power.

The Disconnected Man

I was that man. The disconnected one.

You can know doctrine and still not know yourself.

You can exegete a text and still not excavate your own trauma.

You can serve communion while starving emotionally.

Disconnection was my default.

Most people didn't notice because giftedness is deceptive. We assume it means someone is whole, but it often just means they've learned how to function through the fracture. I wasn't living in sin because I didn't love GOD. I was living in sin because I didn't know how to stop the cycle.

My identity had been shaped by broken images, distorted models, and a theology that emphasized performance over transformation. And it caught up with me, emotionally, relationally, spiritually.

The Unseen Patterns

I wasn't cheating because I didn't love my wife, I was cheating because I didn't love myself. Because I didn't believe healing was for me. Because deep down, I had decided I was destined to struggle, and anything better was a lie.

I had normalized chaos. My threshold for pain was high. I thought brokenness was part of the calling. I wore burnout like a badge and dysfunction like a uniform.

But here's what I've learned: what we normalize in private becomes what we reproduce in public. If your root is damaged, your fruit will be distorted.

Preaching Through Pain

One of the hardest truths I've had to face is that I preached some of my most powerful sermons while bleeding out. I laid hands on people while carrying the weight of unconfessed sin. I led others into freedom while bound by guilt. I also, because of the power differential in the pastor-people relationship sometime manipulated situations. My longing to see people healed and their hearts mended sometimes led to me inserting myself in as "savior" instead of truly introducing them to the SAVIOR.

One thing the preacher often forgets, the man often forgets is the susceptibility to the transfer of issue in their attempt to solve and save. Bishop Noel Jones often mentioned the spiritual openness and vulnerability a preacher has, and I believe it is easily applied to men, after sharing the power of the Gospel. It opens and avails them to the attacks and the access to the very thing they were preaching about or situation they were trying to address.

I remember preaching a conference after a secret relapse, and the Spirit still moved. People shouted. Someone got healed. But afterward, back in the pastor's study, I was so empty I could barely stand.

That's the lie of performance-based ministry, it teaches you to depend on power without presence, gifting without grace, noise without nourishment.

The truth is, the anointing may flow through a cracked vessel, but that doesn't mean the vessel isn't slowly leaking.

From Pulpit to Problem

I got married believing that love would cure lust. That commitment would cancel brokenness. But a ring doesn't erase dysfunction, it exposes it.

My marriage was holy, but I was still haunted. I had not done the work to heal the little boy inside me. The boy who never learned boundaries. The boy who craved affirmation. The boy who feared abandonment and masked it with bravado.

I carried that unhealed boy into my marriage, into my parenting, into my ministry. And no one questioned it, because I was gifted. Because I could "deliver the Word." Because I looked the part.

But looking healed is not the same as being whole.

A Brother's Challenge

One day, I was teaching a preaching class at our National Convention, and I was showing a clip of a lecture by Dr. Mack King Carter. In this lecture, Dr. Carter said this, "You can't preach over your life!" After class, a close friend and college classmate who knew me before and during my marriage pulled me aside. "You can preach," he said, "but can you be present?"

That cut deeper than any altar call.

Presence requires integrity. And integrity means integration, that who I am publicly aligns with who I am privately. That my gifts don't outpace my growth. That my title doesn't become a hiding place.

We talked for hours. He asked hard questions. He didn't let me spiritualize my sin. He reminded me that honesty is holy, and healing requires exposure. That conversation haunted me, but it also helped me.

Therapy and the Theology of Repair

One of the stipulations Karen had after receiving the letters was that we go to marriage counseling. We had tried it before, but I wasn't ready to be healed, so I rejected the sessions under the guise that I felt attacked by the therapist. But, this time was different. I was sick of the carnage that was being caused by me. When my friend made his comment, I realized that the problem wasn't a marital problem as much as it was a Napoleon problem. I also, as a part of my restorative practice for Church was mandated to seek intense psycho-therapy to address what I believed was a Sexual Addiction. I tried several different therapist, but never stuck it out, for I always thought my situation was too tough for them, and possibly that the need for therapy suggested I was weak, faithless, and couldn't fix it myself, but the reality is, I couldn't.

Therapy was not weakness. It was war. Every session was a battle against lies I had believed for decades. Every memory I unpacked felt like surgery, painful, but healing.

I learned about trauma responses. About identity development. About how we form emotional attachments based on early experiences. I realized I had never been equipped to be whole, I had only been trained to appear holy.

Therapy didn't contradict my faith, it deepened it. It revealed that God is not intimidated by our mess. That Jesus didn't die for a performance. He died for the parts we pretend don't exist.

I started tracing roots, how one act of rejection in childhood opened the door to fear. How one buried disappointment led to resentment. How one unchecked pattern became a stronghold. I was taken back to moments of past rejections, especially relational rejection, and realized that the result of those moments of rejection led me to spend the majority of life attempting to seek acceptance and approval. While those moments of rejection seemed minor in my memory, they were actually major in their manifestation. And it was through therapy that the layers got pulled back, and the healing could begin.

And slowly, I began to believe that maybe I wasn't just a problem, I was a person worth saving.

Formed But Not Finished

The mirror didn't break me, it introduced me to my real self.

I wasn't the man people saw on Sunday. I was the man God was still shaping Monday through Saturday. I wasn't defined by my worst decisions, but I was responsible for healing from them.

God doesn't heal what we won't name. And I had spent too long calling activity "anointing," calling sin "struggle," calling trauma "testimony," and calling chaos "calling."

Now, I was ready to be honest. To say: I'm gifted and grieving. I'm anointed and anxious. I'm leading and learning.

That's the paradox of healing: you become more whole the more truth you can carry.

And that's okay. Because God meets us at the mirror, not with shame, but with grace.

Biblical Mirror Moments

I'm not the only one who had a mirror moment.

Adam's mirror wasn't made of glass, it was made of silence. When he sinned, he hid. Covered himself with fig leaves. Tried to shield his shame with something that could never cover the real issue. But God, full of grace and authority, didn't come at him with a sword. He came with a question: *"Where are you?"* That wasn't about geography. It was about honesty. It was an invitation to be seen and saved. But Adam, like so many of us, missed the mirror moment. He blamed. He deflected. He stayed hidden. And in doing so, he forfeited what could've been a path to restoration.

Peter's mirror was a rooster's crow. Bold at dinner. Loud in promise. "I'll never deny You." But in the courtyard, fear overtook faith. And three denials later, the rooster crowed, and Jesus looked at him. Not a look of rage. Not shame. Just truth. Peter wept bitterly, the Bible says. That was his mirror moment. But here's the grace: Jesus didn't discard Peter. He restored him. On a beach, after breakfast, Jesus asked three questions: "Do you love Me?" One for every denial. Not to shame Peter, but to reclaim him.

Adam hid and remained stuck. Peter wept and became a rock.

The question isn't whether you'll have a mirror moment. It's what you'll do with it.

Sidebar: 5 Signs You're Leading While Bleeding

- You avoid silence because you're afraid of what will surface.
- You preach better than you process.
- You confuse applause with acceptance.
- You feel needed but not known.
- You constantly run on empty and call it sacrifice.

If you see yourself here, you're not alone, and you're not beyond repair.

Reflection Questions

- When was the last time you looked at yourself beyond the title?

_____

_____

_____

_____

_____

- What patterns in your life can be traced back to childhood wounds?

_____

_____

_____

_____

_____

- How have you used ministry (or work) to cover unhealed areas?

_____

_____

_____

_____

_____

- What's the difference between performing and becoming?

_____

_____

_____

_____

_____

- What would it mean for you to stop hiding and start healing?

_____

_____

_____

_____

_____

- Who have you hurt because you haven't healed?

_____

_____

_____

_____

_____

- What's one truth you need to name today?

- Who is someone you trust that you can talk to now?

Scripture Meditation
Psalm 51:6
"Behold, you desire truth in the inward parts, and in the hidden part you will make me to know wisdom."

Prayer:

"God, I bring You my reflection. Not just the polished parts, but the broken ones. Help me see what You see. Help me name what I've buried. Help me become who You always intended. Heal me so I can lead from wholeness, not from hiding. Amen."

CHAPTER 2
THE BLUEPRINT WAS BROKEN

Brothers, the truth is, most of us were handed blueprints we never asked for. They weren't drawn in love or sketched in truth. They were scribbled in silence, soaked in shame, and sealed by survival. They came from daddies who disappeared, uncles who deflected, pastors who performed, and big brothers who were broken themselves.

These were handed-down codes of masculinity, inherited instructions on survival, and lessons drawn not from Scripture but from streets, silence, and pain. We were told, "This is what it means to be a man." We inherited these blueprints without questioning them. Because questioning meant being ungrateful. Because naming the problem felt like dishonoring our past. But if the blueprint is broken, the building will be too.

But no one asked: What if the blueprint was broken from the start?

We build our lives according to what we've seen. And for many Black men, especially those called into spiritual leadership, what we've seen hasn't always been whole. We've watched men bury their wounds beneath bravado. We've seen them measure masculinity by dominance and detachment. We've been taught to equate silence with strength and secrecy with protection. And the worst part? We've learned to mistake dysfunction for normalcy.

Broken blueprints become generational blueprints. We inherit not only the trauma but the tools used to hide it.

When I looked at my own life, I realized I wasn't building from GOD's architectural plan, I was stacking bricks on a cracked foundation. What I built looked strong on the outside. But inside, it was hollow, ready to collapse.

This chapter is about confronting the silent contracts we signed with dysfunction. About realizing we were built on broken foundations and that it's not too late to rebuild.

The Formation of a Flawed Framework

Identity doesn't appear out of nowhere, it's formed. And for Black boys growing up in a world that either fears them or fetishizes them, the formation is complicated.

We were formed by:

- Homes where emotions were dangerous
- Churches where holiness meant hiding
- Schools where our anger was punished, but our excellence ignored
- Streets where the only rule was survival

Some of us learned to be men from fathers who were angry, absent, or addicted. Others were raised by strong women who did their best, but were exhausted, and couldn't explain manhood because they had never experienced a whole one.

We formed our identity from what we saw. And too often, what we saw was pain dressed up as pride.

What Was Modeled

As boys, we don't just listen, we absorb. We absorb the conversations, the secrets, the glances, the contradictions. If we saw our fathers cheat, we called it charisma. If we saw our uncles drink their pain away, we called it resilience. If we heard, "Men don't cry," we swallowed our grief and wore a mask.

We copied what we saw because no one showed us a better way.

In many households, especially those led by men who themselves had no blueprint, love was conditional, if spoken at all. Correction was loud, but affirmation was mute. We were taught how to provide, but not how to process. Taught how to fight, but not how to forgive.

We inherited patterns of emotional avoidance. If our dads didn't talk about their failures, neither would we. If our mentors couldn't show weakness, neither could we. We were trained to be emotionally mute but spiritually loud. We learned to function in pulpits and malfunction at home.

The Lie of Strength

We were told strength was silence. That real men didn't cry. That we were to protect and provide, but never process. That as long as we were physically present, emotionally absent didn't matter.

We learned to equate control with maturity. Dominance with power. Lust with love.

And when we entered ministry, we brought those blueprints with us. We thought gifting would override brokenness. That calling would cancel dysfunction. That if we prayed enough, the past would disappear.

But prayer isn't a substitute for processing. Anointing doesn't erase abandonment. And preaching doesn't override pain.

The Culture Complicates It

Culture doesn't just reflect us, it shapes us. And the culture has done a poor job of helping Black men become whole.

We've been told we're only valuable if we perform, if we dominate on the field, deliver in the bedroom, or stack money like a mogul. Our music, our media, even some of our mentors have celebrated hypersexuality, aggression, and emotional detachment.

We cheer for the man who gets revenge, not the one who seeks therapy. We glorify the grind, but never talk about the grief. And then we wonder why so many of us are successful and suicidal, popular and paranoid, influential and internally bleeding.

Even the church has complicated this issue. We've trained preachers how to exegete a passage, but not how to excavate their pain. We've taught pastors to protect the pulpit, but not how to protect their mental health. We've created a theology of perfection, not confession. We have altar calls but no accountability groups. We say, "Be strong in the LORD," but we don't teach how to be soft with our spouse.

And so, our leaders, especially our Black male leaders, are crumbling quietly.

Building on Broken Ground

The problem with building on a faulty foundation is that the cracks will always show, eventually.

We started ministries, families, businesses, dreams, but the base was still unstable. Our ideas about relationships were rooted in control, not covenant. Our views of women were shaped by conquest, not companionship. Our sense of worth was tied to performance, not personhood.

So we built churches but couldn't build trust. We built brands but couldn't build boundaries. We built platforms but couldn't build peace.

Because the blueprint was broken.

Understand my issues were not always sexual in nature, but they were all based on insecurity and uncertainty of my own self. I had low self-esteem and low self-worth, and this meant I was alway seeking outside entities to validate my value. I need the approval of parents and peer. I sought affirmation from classmates and church members. I became performance-driven because performance led to applause and seeming affirmation. I was so busy becoming who

36

I thought would make people happy, that I disconnected from who GOD had created me to be.

What God Actually Designed

Let's go back to the beginning. Genesis doesn't describe a man built to dominate or detach. GOD created Adam in GOD's image, whole, relational, vulnerable, and accountable. Adam walked with GOD in the cool of the day. He wasn't hiding; he was seen. He wasn't dominating; he was naming. He wasn't alone; he was partnered.

That was the original blueprint.

Think about Saul. Chosen by the people. Elevated quickly. But his insecurity was always louder than his anointing. He didn't know how to obey because he had never learned to be obedient to his own story. His kingship was built on fear of man, not fear of GOD.

Or think of Jacob. Grasping from the womb. Always trying to earn a blessing he thought he didn't deserve. His name meant "trickster," and he lived up to it. His blueprint was deceit because his environment taught him that lying was safer than trusting.

Even David, a man after GOD's own heart, struggled with a broken blueprint. He could slay giants but couldn't slay his inner demons. His house was full of chaos because his foundation never taught him how to be present and accountable as a father.

Broken blueprints are not new. But they don't have to be final.

The brokenness we carry didn't come from GOD. It came from the fall. From systems of oppression. From broken homes. From generational pain and cultural confusion. But here's the good news: **GOD's grace doesn't just forgive sin, it heals formation.** GOD doesn't just want to clean up our behavior; He wants to rebuild our identity.

We need to reclaim the blueprint GOD intended, not just for salvation, but for identity, relationships, fatherhood, and leadership.

From Brokenness to Blueprinting Again

Here's what I've learned: healing starts when we stop blaming the bricklayers and start becoming architects.

Yes, we inherited trauma. But we also carry the authority to end it. Yes, our fathers missed it. But our FATHER in heaven models something better. Yes, the church failed to address it. But we are the church, and the church can evolve.

Rebuilding doesn't start with construction, it starts with demolition. We must be willing to:

- Tear down false beliefs about masculinity
- Unlearn toxic theology
- Deconstruct inherited shame

We have to give ourselves permission to feel, to question, to rest, to reimagine.

We are not just builders, we are being rebuilt.

Tearing Down to Rebuild

Rebuilding doesn't start with performance. It starts with demolition, tearing down the false structures built on pride, pain, and protection.

It begins with confession:

- I don't have it all together.
- I don't know how to do this.
- I'm tired of pretending.

We stop blaming our fathers and start healing ourselves. We stop performing for acceptance and start receiving GOD's love as a foundation.

My healing didn't begin in a church service. It began in a therapist's office. It began in silence, in surrender, in journal pages soaked with regret and rediscovery. It began when I admitted that the blueprint I'd been following was leading me to destruction.

That moment was sacred. Not because I had answers. But because I finally admitted I was ready for a better plan.

Cultural Commentary: The Weight of Being a Black Man

The societal blueprint isn't much better. America teaches Black men that our worth is in our work, our wallet, or our woman. That we're threats or trophies, but never tender. That our emotions are either dangerous or irrelevant.

And in ministry, this gets worse. We're taught to be strong for everyone, but rarely are we taught to be safe for ourselves.

That pressure is killing us. We're overrepresented in hypertension, heart disease, and untreated depression. Because the blueprint we were given didn't include care. It included survival.

It's time we redesign.

Reimagining the Blueprint

GOD's blueprint for manhood is one of strength and softness, truth and tenderness, courage and community. JESUS HIMSELF modeled this. HE wept publicly at Lazarus's tomb. HE restored Peter with gentleness. HE carried a cross, yes, but HE also asked, "Can you pray with me?"

So what does a GOD-formed manhood look like?

- It looks like Joseph, who led without manipulation.

- It looks like Moses, who asked for help.
- It looks like Paul, who confessed his thorn.

False manhood says: dominate, suppress, deny. God's blueprint says: love, listen, lead with humility.

We rebuild by telling the truth. By finding mentors who model health. By creating spaces where men can be human, not just heroes.

That's what a man looks like. That's what healing looks like.

So now I build differently. I build with therapy. With prayer. With Scripture. With brothers who hold me accountable. With a wife who doesn't just need my presence, but my truth.

This new foundation isn't flashy. But it's firm.

You can build it too. But first, you've got to admit the old plans have failed.

Reflection Questions

- What blueprints shaped your definition of manhood?

  _____

  _____

  _____

  _____

  _____

- What behaviors have you normalized that are actually rooted in brokenness?

  _____

  _____

  _____

  _____

  _____

- Who are the men you imitated, and what did they teach you about pain?

  _____

  _____

  _____

  _____

  _____

- In what ways has the church failed to teach emotional health alongside spiritual truth?

_____

_____

_____

_____

_____

- What do you think GOD's original design for you actually looks like?

_____

_____

_____

_____

_____

- What parts of your life need to be demolished so something healthier can be built?

_____

_____

_____

_____

_____

Scripture Meditation
Isaiah 58:12
"You shall be called the repairer of the breach, the restorer of streets to dwell in."

Prayer:

"GOD, help me tear down what was built on lies. Teach me how to rebuild with truth, with grace, and with courage. I want YOUR blueprint, not the broken one I was handed. Amen."

CHAPTER 3

THE BROTHER'S BASEMENT – SILENT SCARS, SHARED STRUGGLES

We talk a lot about brotherhood. We celebrate it, tweet about it, preach it. But what happens when brotherhood doesn't heal you, it hides you? What happens when our brotherly bonds become the burial ground for our pain?

The truth is, a lot of us have been gathering in bars, backrooms even barbershops, sunken and secret spaces where we can simply be safe, spiritually, emotionally, mentally. Spaces where we hide our fears and fake our strength. We laugh to cover the trauma. We quote Scripture to silence our suffering. We slap high-fives over heartbreak.

This chapter isn't just about the struggles we've shared, it's about the silence we've signed onto. The unspoken rule that says, "You can be my brother, but don't bring your brokenness." This assumed idea that showing vulnerability and emotion makes one weak or less masculine. So, instead, we pretend. We parade a facade around as if it were our reality. We so want to share what we are really facing. We so want the accountability of someone actually asking us deeper than surface-level questions to shatter the fragile wall we put up.

What we really need is not a place to hide, but we need a place to heal. I want to take this chapter and reimagine the dark spaces as developmental spaces, as deliberate spaces, and as deliverance spaces. I want to welcome my brothers to the BaseMENt.

The BaseMENt is not the lower level of your home, but a place where MEN come and we confront our challenges. It's where we unpack. It's where we begin to rise.

The Unspoken Agreement

Somewhere along the way, many of us made an unspoken pact: we will protect the image, *our image*, at all costs. Don't cry. Don't confess. Don't confront what's really going on. We were celebrated for being strong and silent, suppressing all of our inner emotions until they could no longer be contained.

We learned to:

Laugh at trauma

Like *Marcus*, who tells the story at every cookout about the time his mom threw his sneakers and clothes into the yard during a fight with her boyfriend. He performs it so well, voices, gestures, and all, that the whole family howls with laughter, never realizing the humiliation he felt in that moment.

Just like *Richard Pryor*, who built his career on jokes about his abusive, chaotic childhood, making people laugh while his personal life crumbled under addiction and pain. Both learned to turn their trauma into entertainment, because laughter felt safer than silence.

Dress up dysfunction

Like *David*, who never misses church in his perfectly pressed suit. People call him "sharp" and ask him for advice, but nobody knows his marriage is in shambles, his kids don't speak to him, and his credit cards are maxed out.

Just like *Malcolm X*, who before his transformation was "Detroit Red", always the most polished man in the room, using his style and charm to mask his anger, his hustles, and his brokenness. Both mastered the art of looking good while falling apart.

Normalize numbness

Like *Jamal*, who hasn't cried since his brother was murdered when he was 16. He goes through life saying, *"It is what it is,"* whether he's burying a loved one, losing a job, or watching his marriage unravel, feelings locked away behind a stone face.

Just like *Mike Tyson*, who admitted he didn't cry when his mother died because he simply didn't know how anymore, his heart already hardened by years of violence and loss.

Both learned that shutting down emotions was the only way to keep moving forward.

We became brothers in arms, but not brothers in healing.

We knew how to talk about sports, strategy, and even Scripture, but not about shame. Not about being touched too early. Or growing up without a father. Or hating what we see in the mirror.

This silence wasn't strength, it was survival. But survival is not the same as healing.

The Psychology of Silence

Silence isn't always strength. Sometimes it's trauma wearing a tuxedo.

Many of us learned to keep quiet because talking got you punished. Emotions made you look weak. Crying meant you weren't "man enough." Over time, that silence became self-defense, and self-defense turned into self-destruction.

In the absence of expression, pain festers. Secrets grow. Shame deepens. And before you know it, you've got men preaching deliverance while secretly bound, teaching forgiveness while nursing old wounds.

We were taught to "man up," but not to open up. To provide, but not to process. The pressure to always be strong has left us emotionally starved.

Silence doesn't protect us. It imprisons us, and as leaders and preachers, and parents, it ends up harming those who follow us, depend on us, look up to us, and try to emulate us. We end up modeling the very mess we are going through, and they assume our dysfunction is deliberate and desired. They become our brokenness.

The Danger of Leading While Wounded

Ministry doesn't pause for your pain. Sunday comes whether your heart is healed or not. And that's the danger. We keep going. We keep performing. We spiritualize burnout and call it perseverance. We confuse being needed with being whole.

But unaddressed wounds leak. Into our sermons. Our marriages. Our children. Our self-esteem. Our theology. Even sadder is we are carrying the baggage alone. We are leaking alone.

But where do we go to address it? How can we unpack the pain we are carrying? Can this be the best GOD has for us? This is how sabotage suffocates us. We lose hope of healing and hold on to our hurt like it's our trophy or like it's our testimony.

When we normalize silent suffering, we sabotage long-term health.

Reimagining the Basement

Many of us grew up without safe spaces to feel. We were told to "man up," to stop crying, to suck it up. And so for many of us, the basement, literal or figurative, became the place we hid.

The place we numbed out with pills or pornography.

The place we buried our dreams after one failure.

The place we watched others succeed while quietly feeling like impostors.

Even when we gathered in the same rooms, we were suffering alone.

But what if the basement didn't have to stay that way?

What if we could turn it into something else?

Finding the BaseMENt

There's a room beneath the sanctuary where the truth lives. Not the pulpit. Not the pew. Not the green room.

I'm talking about the **BaseMENt**, the Brother's BaseMENt.

That's the space where clergy collars loosen, voices soften, and the real stories start to flow.

It's where the question isn't, *"How big is your church?"* but, *"Are you okay?"* It's where brothers take off the masks, where no one flinches when you say, *"I'm bleeding too."*

In that low place, I felt something holy, not the performance of church, but the presence of brotherhood.

The BaseMENt became a space to be whole, not because we had all the answers, but because we finally started asking better questions.

And what if we didn't stop there?

What if the spaces we ran to for shelter, barbershops, locker rooms, corners, became places we could actually seek help? What if the barbershop became the **Bettershop**, where cuts came with counsel, and fades came with freedom?

What if locker rooms became listening rooms?

What if corners became circles, and hiding places became healing places?

The BaseMENt is not just a room, it's a reimagining.

It's a renovation of the spaces we once used to avoid our pain into spaces that help us face it.

It's where we move from just being brothers in arms... to becoming brothers in healing.

From Isolation to Interdependence

The opposite of isolation isn't a crowd, it's community.

True brotherhood is not built on ego or platform. It's built on truth. Confession. Accountability. Grace. In the BaseMENt, we wouldn't offer each other cheap advice. We offered presence. We held space.

Some of the most powerful healing moments in my life didn't happen at the altar, they happened in between sobs, when another man said, "I get it. I've been there."

I remember sitting in a circle with men I admired, pastors, leaders, husbands. All of us gifted. All of us exhausted. And for the first time, we told the truth.

One brother admitted to infidelity. Another to suicidal thoughts. Another to numbing himself with success.

And instead of judging, we leaned in. We prayed. We cried. We held each other up.

When you know you're not the only one bleeding, you stop being ashamed of your scars. And when you stop hiding your scars, they become testimonies.

That night didn't fix everything. But it changed everything. Because it proved what I now believe to be true:

Confession is the doorway to community. And community is the doorway to healing.

A Word from My Own BaseMENt

My community, my BaseMENt wasn't found at church, but it was made up of people from "church". My community was created around the firepit after the convention or convocation and it was convened over cigars. I met a group of men who had walked through fire. Preachers who had been divorced. Pastors battling addiction. Ministers silently fighting depression. These were not weak men. They were gifted, powerful, called men. But they were human, and they were hurting.

One by one, we shared. And one by one, we discovered we weren't alone.

There's power in shared struggle. Not just to commiserate, but to confess. Not just to weep, but to work through it. The BaseMENt gave us permission to be honest without fear of losing credibility.

Too often, leaders don't get that. We're expected to bleed quietly. To preach through pain. To counsel while crumbling. But in the BaseMENt, we weren't expected to perform. We were expected to be present.

Real men, real tears, real healing.

Shared Struggles, Shared Strength

The same place where pain is shared can also be the place where power is rediscovered. Strength isn't just about standing tall, it's about staying connected.

Think of David. When he ran to the cave of Adullam, he wasn't hiding alone. Other distressed, indebted, and discontented men came to him. That cave became a brotherhood, and from it, David's mighty men were born (1 Samuel 22:1-2). It started with brokenness. But it didn't end there.

Think of Jesus in Gethsemane. He didn't go alone. He took Peter, James, and John. Even the Son of God wanted company in His agony. His request wasn't for solutions, just presence. "Watch and pray with Me."

Strength isn't the absence of pain, it's the refusal to face it alone.

And historically, some of the strongest movements began with shared vulnerability. The Civil Rights Movement wasn't birthed in boardrooms, it grew from basements and back rooms, barber shops and fellowship halls, where Black men dared to share their dreams, doubts, and strategies. Where they dared to cry, to pray, and to plan.

There's something powerful about hearing a brother say, "Me too." Not as a punchline, but as a promise: You're not crazy. You're not alone. You're not beyond redemption.

Shared struggle doesn't mean shared solutions. But it does mean shared safety. It creates the space to say:

- "I still have trust issues."
- "I've battled addiction."
- "I've failed my wife and didn't think I'd recover."

And in those confessions, healing begins.

Because what we confess, we can confront. And what we confront, we can change.

Building a New Brotherhood

We don't need more critics. We need brothers who will:

- Check in, not just cheer us on
- Tell the truth, not just preach it
- Hold us accountable, not hostage
- Remind us that healing is a journey, not a performance

The Brother's BaseMENt isn't about weakness. It's about wisdom. It's about building safe spaces where honesty is holy and healing is possible.

Imagine if every pastor, every leader, every father had a basement, a brotherhood below the stage. A space beneath the spotlight. A circle beyond the crowd.

Let's build more basements. Let's be brave enough to descend so we can rise again.

What if we built something new? What if our brotherhood was based on:

- Presence, not perfection
- Confession, not competition
- Healing, not hiding

What if the next time we gathered, we asked real questions?

- "What's heavy right now?"
- "What lie are you still believing about yourself?"
- "What's one truth you need to hear from a brother today?"

And what if we didn't just ask, but stayed long enough to listen?

True brotherhood is not built in performance. It's built in presence.

Imagine Your Own BaseMENt

So what about you?

Where is *your* BaseMENt?

Where could you go, or who could you go to, to take off the armor? To speak the truth?

What would it look like to repurpose your hiding place into a healing place?

Close your eyes and picture it:

- Who's in the room with you?

- What does it sound like when you finally say what you've been holding back?

- How does it feel when someone looks at you, not with judgment, but with love, and says, *"Me too."*

Your BaseMENt can start wherever you're willing to be real.

And you don't have to build it alone.

Reflection Questions

- Who are the men in your life that know your truth, not just your title?

_____

_____

_____

_____

_____

- Where have you been bleeding silently, and why?

_____

_____

_____

_____

_____

- Have you confused isolation with strength? How has that hurt you?

_____

_____

_____

_____

_____

- What would a healing community look like for you?

  _____

  _____

  _____

  _____

  _____

- Who are 1–2 brothers you trust enough to invite into your BaseMENt?

  _____

  _____

  _____

  _____

  _____

- What space in your life could be reimagined as a healing space, a barbershop, a locker room, a group chat, a backyard?

  _____

  _____

  _____

  _____

  _____

- What's the first question you would want someone to ask you in that space?

_____

_____

_____

_____

_____

- What's the first truth you need to say out loud in that space?

_____

_____

_____

_____

_____

Scripture Meditation
James 5:16
"Confess your faults one to another, and pray for one another, that ye may be healed."

Prayer:

"GOD, thank You for the brothers who see me beyond my title. Help me create and cherish spaces of truth, vulnerability, and healing. GOD, I'm tired of hiding in the basement. Bring me into a community that sees me, hears me, and holds me accountable. Teach me how to lead while leaning on others. Make me a safe space, and surround me with the same, not shame. And let healing begin with me. Amen."

SECTION ONE SUMMARY

NAMING THE WOUND

Before healing can begin, the wound must be named.

Section One invited us into a sacred reckoning, a bold, painful, necessary confrontation with our stories. It was the descent into the basement, the peeling back of public polish to expose private pain. We didn't hide behind titles. We told the truth behind the talent.

We explored what it means to look in the mirror and see a mess, not as condemnation, but as invitation. We named what was broken in the blueprint we were handed. We exposed the silent agreements we've made with shame, secrecy, and survival. And we stepped into the basement, not just to bleed, but to be seen and to begin again.

In Chapter 1, we owned the reality that performing and pretending are no substitutes for presence and peace.

In Chapter 2, we examined how broken blueprints become generational strongholds, and what it means to rebuild from God's original design.

In Chapter 3, we entered the brother's basement, where silence was shattered, stories were shared, and strength was rediscovered in community.

Section One didn't fix it all, but it told the truth. And truth is the beginning of transformation.

Now, we pivot.

In Section Two, we begin the work of restoration, not with hustle, but with healing. We move from naming the wound to renewing the identity. We look again at who we were from the beginning, not who the world, our wounds, or our saboteurs told us to be.

Let's begin to rebuild.

SECTION TWO

FROM WOUNDS TO WISDOM – HEALING THE MAN WITHIN

There comes a moment in every man's life when survival stops being enough. When titles, talents, and traditions can no longer quiet the deep ache beneath the surface.

In Section One, we named the pain, exposing the wounds, broken blueprints, hidden BaseMENts, and sabotage scripts that kept us stuck.

Now, we go deeper.

This section is about reclaiming the man beneath the mask.

It's where we stop rehearsing our dysfunction and start reimagining our design.

Here, we learn a new language for manhood, one rooted in healing, accountability, and authenticity.

We unlearn the performance and embrace the process.

We give ourselves permission to feel, to question, and to hope again.

We move from trauma-informed silence to Spirit-empowered truth.

We move from being managed by our mess to being mentored by our healing.

We move from wounds to wisdom.

Let's begin the work of becoming whole.

CHAPTER 4

SABOTAGE SCRIPTS – WHEN THE LIES SOUND LIKE TRUTH

Every man has a script playing in the background of his mind.

It's not always loud. Sometimes it sounds like your own voice. Sometimes it mimics the voice of your father, a coach, a pastor, or a past partner. These scripts shape how you see yourself, how you love, how you lead, how you live. And far too often, the script is a lie, but it's been rehearsed for so long, it feels like truth.

This chapter is about those lies. About the messages we've internalized that sabotage our success, our relationships, our wholeness. It's about identifying the scripts we didn't write but somehow memorized, and choosing to rewrite them.

Let me be honest: I've performed with power while privately panicking. I've quoted Scriptures on wholeness while silently unraveling. And I've smiled in public while drowning in private. The script I had memorized was this: "If they ever find out who you really are, it's over." That script kept me bound in cycles I never thought I'd survive. But thank God for grace that exposes to heal, not to humiliate.

What's a Sabotage Script?

A sabotage script is a recurring thought, belief, or emotional loop that keeps you stuck. It's not just negative self-talk. It's deeper. It's the internalized shame, fear, and falsehood that shows up whenever you're about to break through.

Sabotage scripts sound like:

- "I'm only valuable when I perform."
- "If I'm not perfect, I'll be rejected."
- "I can't trust anyone with my truth."
- "I'll always mess it up eventually."
- "I have to stay strong or everything will fall apart."

They are inherited, reinforced, and repeated. And they are deadly. They disguise themselves as protection but often function as prison walls.

Sometimes they come wrapped in religion: "God only uses clean vessels." Sometimes they come cloaked in culture: "Real men don't show emotion." Either way, they sabotage intimacy, identity, and even our ability to receive grace.

These scripts don't just show up in crisis, they are embedded in our everyday choices: how we apologize, how we love, how we hustle, how we hide.

Where Do They Come From?

Some scripts come from trauma, words spoken in moments of pain. Some come from silence, what was never said to affirm us. Others come from culture, what masculinity, success, or spirituality *should* look like.

We absorbed them from:

- Fathers who were present in body but absent in affirmation
- Church leaders who preached perfection but modeled pretense
- Relationships where vulnerability was punished

- Environments where feelings were forbidden

And let's be real: the world doesn't disciple men to be whole. It teaches us to perform, produce, and protect at all costs, even when our souls are starving. We are taught to dominate, but not to be discerning. To conquer, but not to connect. To grind, but not to grieve.

Sometimes the most powerful scripts are not what was said, but what was never said at all. The "you'll never be good enough" wasn't always verbalized. It was felt in the looks, in the withdrawal, in the unmet need for affirmation.

The tragedy is that we adopted survival tactics that no longer serve us. What kept us safe as boys is now suffocating us as men.

The Cost of Internalized Lies

Every time we repeat these scripts, we reinforce a prison. They sabotage:

- Intimacy ("I can't let her see the real me.")
- Opportunity ("I'm not good enough to lead that.")
- Creativity ("They'll laugh if I fail.")
- Healing ("I don't deserve to be whole.")

They make us shrink in rooms where we should stand tall. They cause us to settle when we should stretch. They keep us from asking for help because they convince us it's a weakness.

They drive us to burnout and call it work ethic. They make us chase applause while running from authenticity. They tell us vulnerability is dangerous, when in fact it's the doorway to connection.

And here's the danger: What goes unchallenged becomes a standard. These lies get passed down to sons and taught to mentees. Without healing, we normalize self-sabotage and call it leadership.

Unchallenged scripts become lifelong strongholds. But strongholds can be broken.

The Day I Believed the Lie

I'll never forget the day of my ordination, standing in the sanctuary of my home church, dressed in my suit and standing with my family, four months after finishing seminary, and being appointed as Pastor of Christian Education and Missions.

On paper, I was ready. I was the only one on that platform with a Master of Divinity. I had done the work, late nights, long prayers, countless papers. But as I stood there, surrounded by the same people who had watched me grow up, all I could feel was the weight of their whispers.

"He's too young… it's just favoritism… he's not ready…"

And because of my flaws and peculiarities, the parts of me that never quite fit their mold, I believed them.

I smiled for the pictures. I gave the right answers. But inside, I was crumbling. Every handshake, every "Congratulations" sounded like a dare: *Let's see how long before you prove them right.*

That day, the script that played in my head was this: *"You're only here because they don't see the real you, and when they do, it's over."*

It was imposter syndrome in full force. Not because I wasn't prepared, but because I had learned to measure my worth by other people's acceptance.

But here's what I've learned since then: the moment you name that lie out loud, the moment you stop pretending and start telling the truth about what you feel, the healing begins.

That's the power of light: it breaks the hold of the lie.

If you're willing to name it, GOD is faithful to rewrite it.

Rewriting the Script

You can't cast out what you won't confront. And you can't heal what you won't name.

Let's make this practical. Start here:

- Identify the Lie – What falsehood are you believing about yourself?

- Trace the Origin – When and where did this lie take root?

- Declare the Truth – What does GOD actually say about you?

- Create a New Narrative – Write the script you *want* to believe and practice it daily.

Rewrite Worksheet

- Old Script: _____

- Where it Came From: _____

- Truth from Scripture: _____

- My New Script: _____

Example

- Old Script: "I am too broken to be used."

- Origin: Church discipline after a moral failure.

- Truth: "My grace is sufficient for you, for my power is made perfect in weakness." (2 Cor. 12:9)

- New Script: "I am a vessel of grace, not because I am flawless, but because God is faithful."

Write your script. Speak it aloud. Repeat it until it becomes your new default.

Biblical Examples of Sabotage Scripts

Moses: "I can't speak well."

When GOD called Moses to lead Israel out of Egypt, Moses protested: *"I am slow of speech and of tongue"* (Exodus 4:10). His script

67

was **insecurity**, convinced his flaws disqualified him from his calling. But GOD didn't abandon him; instead, HE equipped him, sending Aaron to stand alongside him and proving that HIS power is made perfect even through trembling lips.

Gideon: "I'm the least in my family."

When the Angel of the LORD called Gideon to deliver Israel, Gideon argued: *"My clan is the weakest in Manasseh, and I am the least in my family"* (Judges 6:15). His script was **inferiority**, defining himself by his family's status and his own perceived insignificance. But GOD called him *mighty warrior* before he even swung a sword, showing that identity comes from HIS word, not our rank.

Peter: "Depart from me, I'm a sinful man."

After witnessing Jesus' miraculous catch of fish, Peter fell at HIS knees and confessed: *"Go away from me, Lord; I am a sinful man!"* (Luke 5:8). His script was **shame**, overwhelmed by his failures and convinced he was unworthy of closeness to Christ. But JESUS ignored his shame, calling him instead to follow and become a shepherd of souls, proving that grace writes a new story.

Paul: "I have a thorn."

Paul, the apostle, spoke of a mysterious "thorn in the flesh" that tormented him (2 Corinthians 12:7–9). He begged for it to be removed, seeing it as a weakness, his script was **unworthiness and limitation**. Yet GOD's response was not to take the thorn away but to reveal a deeper truth: *"My grace is sufficient for you, for My power is made perfect in weakness."* Paul discovered that what he thought disqualified him was the very place where GOD's glory shined brightest.

GOD never waited for their scripts to change before HE used them. But HE did confront their lies to heal them.

That's the gospel, it reaches you in the middle of your lie, and then it walks you step by step toward the truth.

Identifying Your Saboteur

We all have that voice in our head.

You know the one, the voice that tells you, *"You're not enough,"* or *"You're going to mess this up,"* or *"You'd better stay in control because nobody else will."*

For years, I thought it was just me, just part of my personality. But I've learned that voice has a name.

Psychologist Shirzad Chamine, in his Positive Intelligence framework, identifies ten internal Saboteurs, mental habits and emotional reflexes that sabotage your peace, performance, and potential. These inner critics may sound like self-protection, but they lead to cycles of shame, avoidance, control, and disconnection.

Here are the ten saboteurs:

- The Judge: Constantly criticizes you and others; the root of all saboteurs.

  Example: You land a promotion but instantly downplay your success: "They only gave it to me because of a quota." You struggle to celebrate yourself. Here is how it may also play out. Marcus is a pastor who secretly believes he's a fraud. After every sermon, he replays what he said, criticizing every word. When others affirm him, he deflects it, convinced they just don't know the "real him." Internally, he feels like he's never enough, even to God.

- The Controller: Needs to take charge and dominate situations to feel safe.

  Example: You lead everything, from the ministry to your family, because trusting others feels like vulnerability. You believe, "If I don't do it, it won't get done right." Here is how it may also play out. Devon leads a men's ministry and runs his household like a military base. He doesn't delegate because he fears losing control. Underneath, he's terrified of vulnerability. Control is how he keeps from feeling out of control like he did growing up in an unstable home.

- The Stickler: A perfectionist obsessed with order and doing things the "right" way.

  Example: You spend hours re-editing sermons or projects, paralyzed by the fear that someone might critique your excellence, especially in white-dominated spaces. Here is how it also may play out. Omar obsesses over every detail when preparing for a church conference. When volunteers make mistakes, he micromanages or redoes the work himself. His perfectionism makes him difficult to work with and leaves him isolated, even though he longs for team connection.

- The Pleaser: Seeks acceptance by pleasing others at the expense of self.

  Example: You say yes to every church duty and community request, even when you're exhausted, afraid that saying no might make you appear ungrateful or selfish. Here is how it also may play out. Anthony says yes to every request, preaching, counseling, mentoring, because he doesn't want to disappoint anyone. When he's overwhelmed, he suffers in silence. He equates love with being useful and fears abandonment if he ever stops showing up.

- The Hyper-Achiever: Bases self-worth on performance and external success.

  Example: You feel empty unless you're receiving praise, awards, or speaking invitations. When you're not achieving, you feel invisible. Here's how it also may show up. Jamal is a high-profile community leader with accolades and media recognition. But deep down, he's empty. Without success or applause, he feels invisible. Every achievement becomes another mask over his unresolved childhood shame.

- The Victim: Feels misunderstood and uses emotional intensity for validation.

Example: You quietly suffer but hope others will notice your pain without you having to speak up. When they don't, you withdraw, convinced no one really cares. Here's another way it show up. Leon grew up being overlooked. Now, even in leadership, he withdraws emotionally when he feels misunderstood. He longs for affirmation but doesn't know how to ask. He often spirals into self-pity and assumes no one truly sees his heart.

- The Hyper-Rational: Disconnects from emotion and over-values logic.

  Example: You dismiss your partner's feelings as "dramatic" or "illogical" and rely solely on intellect in arguments, struggling to access or name your own emotions. Here's another way it may show up. Quincy leads with logic and scripture but avoids emotional conversations. When his wife cries, he shuts down or quotes Bible verses instead of offering comfort. Emotions feel unsafe, so he intellectualizes every problem, even his pain.

- The Hyper-Vigilant: Sees the world as full of threats; lives in constant anxiety.

  Example: You check your rearview mirror multiple times on the way home, not just from police, but from the pressure of always being watched, critiqued, or judged. Here's another way it may show up. Darius constantly scans for threats, criticism, betrayal, or failure. Growing up in tough neighborhoods and hostile churches taught him to stay on edge. Even in moments of peace, he expects the worst, living in quiet anxiety.

- The Restless: Always chasing the next thing, unable to stay present.

  Example: You jump from one vision, job, or ministry to another, telling yourself it's about growth, but really, it's about escaping stillness and the pain that comes with it. Here's how else it shows up. Chris can't sit still. He's always launching something, another podcast, another program, another service. When asked to rest, he deflects. Productivity keeps him from facing deeper issues he's not ready to name.

- The Avoider: Escapes conflict and uncomfortable emotions.

  Example: You refuse to confront a toxic friend or ministry leader because you'd rather "keep the peace," even though that peace is eating you alive. Here's another way it may show up. Terrence knows his church is toxic, but he won't confront the dysfunction. He avoids hard conversations with his team and pacifies conflict with over-spiritualization. Avoidance has kept the peace, but it's killing his passion.

These multiple conversation-partners either mix together or individually influence us through the manipulation of our minds and manifest in multiple ways that keep us from being our best self. Did any of these sound familiar? I encourage you to stop right now, and take the saboteur assessment for yourself. Find out which one or ones are in conversation with your performance and your person, so that we can move to reforming and removing them from the conversation.

Take the Saboteur Assessment: Want to identify your top saboteurs? Visit https://www.positiveintelligence.com/saboteurs

A New Script for the Sons

Imagine a new internal narrative:

- "I am not my failure."
- "I can be honest and still be strong."
- "God loves me fully, before I fix myself."
- "I am enough, and I'm becoming more."

Healing begins when we replace condemnation with compassion.

Speaking truth aloud, especially in the face of deeply rehearsed lies, is an act of holy resistance. When you say, "I am not what happened to me, I am what I choose to heal," you are beginning a revolution inside your own soul.

What We've Named, We Can Heal

You've named the noise. You've confronted the scripts. You've exposed the saboteurs. That is no small thing. That is sacred work. Before we move forward into healing, identity reformation, and wholeness, pause here and acknowledge what you've just done: you have looked your past and your patterns in the face, and told the truth.

Now, let's turn the corner. We've uncovered the wound. In the next section, we begin the work of healing it.

Reflection Questions

- What lie has shaped how you see yourself?

_____

_____

_____

_____

_____

- When did you first hear or believe that lie?

_____

_____

_____

_____

_____

- How has that script limited your growth, intimacy, or faith?

_____

_____

_____

_____

_____

- What truth from GOD's Word directly contradicts it?

  _____

  _____

  _____

  _____

  _____

- What would your life look like if you believed that truth?

  _____

  _____

  _____

  _____

  _____

- Who do you trust to walk with you as you replace the old script?

  _____

  _____

  _____

  _____

  _____

Scripture Meditation
Romans 12:2
"Be transformed by the renewing of your mind."

Prayer:

"GOD, reveal the scripts I've rehearsed that are rooted in lies. Expose the sabotage I've accepted as normal. Replace every false narrative with Your truth. Give me the courage to rewrite my story with grace, truth, and hope. Amen."

CHAPTER 5

UNLEARNING SURVIVAL – THE COST OF HUSTLING WHILE HURTING

I thought hustle made me holy. If I stayed busy enough, maybe God wouldn't notice how broken I was. Maybe if I kept grinding, no one would see how much I was grieving. I preached about grace while secretly believing that rest was a luxury I hadn't earned. I wore exhaustion like a badge. I mistook busyness for purpose, and performance for identity.

But the truth is, hustle is a mask, and I wore it well.

This chapter is about the lie of survival. It's about the internalized belief that being always-on, always-producing, always-rescuing is somehow a sign of worth. It's about how hustle culture, even in ministry, becomes a trauma response. And more than that, it's about learning to live differently. Learning to rest. Learning to receive. Learning to reclaim the identity God gave us before we ever did a single thing to earn it.

"Self-sabotage by definition is the act of consciously or unconsciously hindering your own success or happiness... It is an intrinsic, individual act done by yourself to yourself and things attached to yourself, your family, your future, your finances."

Before we can reform identity, we must admit the ways we've distorted or diminished it. For many of us, self-sabotage has become the echo beneath our efforts. We wear productivity like armor while silently participating in our own undoing. But God didn't design us to sabotage our way through life, He designed us to live from the fullness of who we are.

Survival Is Not Your Calling

Many of us grew up thinking survival was strength. That grinding was godliness. That if we kept performing, we'd eventually arrive at wholeness. But survival is not the same as healing. You can't heal while pretending you don't hurt.

Survival taught us:

- Don't stop or you'll fall apart.
- Don't rest or someone will replace you.
- Don't feel or you'll lose control.

We internalized hustle as holiness because the alternative, stillness, felt dangerous. Stillness made space for pain. And we didn't know what to do with that.

But survival has a cost. It numbs you to joy. It isolates you from intimacy. It erodes your ability to hear God's voice clearly.

What if God never called you to hustle your way into healing? What if your greatest breakthrough starts with rest?

SIDEBAR: Hustle vs. Holy – Rewriting the Script (In a chart)

Hustle Lie	Holy Truth
If I slow down, I'll fall behind.	Rest is a part of divine rhythm.
If I stop serving, they won't love me.	You are loved apart from your labor.

If I'm not achieving, I'm not worthy.	Your worth is rooted in your identity.
If I fail, I'll lose everything.	Failure is a teacher, not a tombstone.

How We Built Our Identity on the Grind

For years, my value was measured by what I could do, how many people I could serve, how many sermons I could preach, how many hours I could work, and how many degrees I could get. I was a performer. Rest was for other people. I was the fixer, the go-to, the strong one.

But beneath the grind was grief. Behind the productivity was pain. I was hiding behind my calendar so I didn't have to confront my soul.

So many men have built identities on what they can produce instead of who they are.

- Your job title isn't your identity.
- Your sexual conquest isn't your confidence.
- Your spiritual gifting isn't your worth.

When your identity is tied to doing, you will always be one mistake, one failure, one lost opportunity away from collapse. And the enemy loves that. He doesn't have to destroy you if he can just keep you distracted.

But healing begins when you stop running.

Let me tell you about a brother named Darren. A brilliant preacher. Dynamic communicator. Always on. But when he stopped to breathe, really breathe, he admitted he didn't know who he was apart from a microphone. Hustle had given him visibility, but it had stolen his vulnerability. He was well-known, but unknown to himself.

What Self-Sabotage Really Costs

I didn't understand how expensive survival could be. It cost me rest. It cost me trust. It cost me the ability to feel joy.

I wasn't just burning out, I was burning bridges. When we hustle for healing, we end up with crowds that cheer our performance but never know our pain. And deep down, that kind of isolation is unbearable.

The Example of Jesus

Jesus wasn't in a hurry. He wasn't anxious about proving His worth. Before He performed a single miracle, God spoke over Him: "This is my beloved Son, in whom I am well pleased." (Matthew 3:17)

Beloved before the miracles. Approved before the ministry. Secure before the struggle.

If Jesus needed rest, so do you. If Jesus could walk away from crowds, you can say no. If Jesus prayed in lonely places, you don't have to fear solitude.

He didn't equate silence with rejection. He didn't confuse activity with anointing. He operated from identity, not for it.

We need that model. A manhood that makes space for presence over performance. That honors quiet over chaos. That roots identity in being before doing.

From Saboteur to Sage – Activating the Counter Voice

We spent the last chapter really engaging with those Saboteurs. Those negative internal conversation partners that challenge, confront and often conquer our ability to be all that we were created to be. Before we explore how the Sage counters sabotage, let's name the five Sage Powers defined in Shirzad Chamine's Positive Intelligence framework. Each one is rooted in wisdom, and when activated, these voices quiet the chaos and amplify healing:

1. Empathize – Brings compassion to the places we would usually criticize.

2. Explore – Encourages curiosity instead of judgment.

3. Innovate – Imagines new, grace-filled alternatives.

4. Navigate – Aligns us with our values and true purpose.

5. Activate – Propels us into courageous, clear action.

These Sage Powers are not about spiritual bypassing, they are about accessing the Spirit-led voice that says, "There is still a better way."

Let's now revisit our saboteur case studies with the Sages guiding the conversation...

Marcus (The Judge)

Saboteur Lens: Marcus is a pastor who secretly believes he's a fraud. After every sermon, he replays what he said, criticizing every word. When others affirm him, he deflects it, convinced they just don't know the "real him." Internally, he feels like he's never enough, even to God.

Sage Response:

- Empathize: Marcus takes a breath and speaks to the younger version of himself, the boy who was only praised for performing well. He says, *"You don't have to earn your right to be loved. Even in your flaws, you are worthy of grace."*

- Explore: He asks, *"When did I first believe I wasn't enough?"* As he traces that belief back to an overly critical childhood home, he begins to loosen the grip of shame.

- Innovate: Marcus imagines preaching not to impress, but to connect. He experiments with moments of vulnerability in his sermons, sharing parts of his story and letting people see the human side of ministry.

- Navigate: He realigns his motivations, preaching not for validation but for transformation. He prays, *"God, help me to speak from truth, not insecurity."*

- Activate: After the next sermon, Marcus accepts compliments with a simple "thank you." He resists the urge to critique himself to death. Instead, he journals what felt honest and Spirit-led, and chooses to celebrate progress, not perfection.

Devon (The Controller)

Saboteur Lens: Devon leads a men's ministry and runs his household like a military base. He doesn't delegate because he fears losing control. Underneath, he's terrified of vulnerability. Control is how he keeps from feeling out of control like he did growing up in an unstable home.

Sage Response:

- Empathize: Devon reflects on the younger version of himself who had to grow up fast in a chaotic household. He speaks gently to that inner boy: *"You're safe now. You don't have to carry it all by yourself anymore."*

- Explore: He asks himself, *"When did I first learn that control equals safety?"* He remembers watching his father's unpredictable moods and vowing never to feel helpless again. Naming that fear unlocks the ability to examine it with grace, not guilt.

- Innovate: Devon tries a new approach. Instead of controlling every event, he empowers his ministry team to make key decisions. He experiments with trust as a leadership tool and begins to see growth in places where micromanagement used to stunt development.

- Navigate: In prayer and journaling, Devon identifies his true values: stability, protection, and growth. He realizes that those values can still be honored, but through collaboration, not control.

- Activate: Devon starts delegating with intentionality. He holds space for feedback and invites others to lead beside him, not behind him. He even asks his wife how she feels about his leadership at home, and listens without defense.

Omar (The Stickler)

Saboteur Lens: Omar obsesses over every detail when preparing for a church conference. When volunteers make mistakes, he micromanages or redoes the work himself. His perfectionism makes him difficult to work with and leaves him isolated, even though he longs for team connection.

Sage Response:

- Empathize: Omar reflects on his childhood, where he was praised only when things were perfect. He tells his younger self, *"You were doing your best to be seen. You don't have to earn love through flawless execution anymore."*

- Explore: He pauses and asks, *"What do I fear will happen if I let others take the lead?"* He realizes he fears being blamed or abandoned. By naming that fear, he can now walk with it instead of hiding behind it.

- Innovate: Omar experiments with letting others take ownership of their tasks. He encourages creative input from team members and shifts from control to collaboration, slowly discovering that shared excellence is possible, and often better.

- Navigate: He reflects on his values: excellence, integrity, and empowerment. He recognizes that micromanaging violates all three by eroding trust and limiting others' growth. He commits to valuing process over perfection.

- Activate: During the next project, Omar intentionally affirms volunteers publicly, even when things aren't done "his way." He invites feedback and starts leading with grace, not fear. He begins to enjoy ministry again, not for how perfect it looks, but for how present he feels in it.

Anthony (The Pleaser)

Saboteur Lens: Anthony says yes to every request, preaching, counseling, mentoring, because he doesn't want to disappoint anyone. When he's overwhelmed, he suffers in silence. He equates love with being useful and fears abandonment if he ever stops showing up.

Sage Response:

- Empathize: Anthony takes a quiet moment to say to himself, *"You don't have to earn love by exhausting yourself. You are valuable even when you're unavailable."* He remembers how, as a child, affirmations only came after achievements, and offers that little boy some long-overdue grace.

- Explore: He asks himself, *"What am I afraid will happen if I say no?"* Through journaling, he traces it back to being abandoned emotionally by a parent who only engaged when he performed. He realizes his yes is often rooted in a fear of being left behind.

- Innovate: Anthony practices a new approach, he starts suggesting boundaries with options: "I can't preach this Sunday, but I can meet with you next week." He begins creating templates of response that reflect availability without overextending.

- Navigate: He revisits his core values: integrity, sustainability, and presence. He recognizes that constant availability violates all three. He reflects, *"If I collapse from burnout, I can't serve anyone, including God."*

- Activate: Anthony speaks with his ministry team and creates a weekly rhythm that includes rest, reflection, and relationship. He even adds a recurring reminder in his phone: "Love isn't earned by sacrifice, it's received through presence."

Jamal (The Hyper-Achiever)

Saboteur Lens: Jamal is a high-profile community leader with accolades and media recognition. But deep down, he's empty. Without success or applause, he feels invisible. Every achievement becomes another mask over his unresolved childhood shame.

Sage Reframe:

- Empathize: Jamal acknowledges the little boy inside him who only felt seen when he brought home trophies. He places a hand on his chest, breathing deep, saying, *"You matter even when no one's clapping."*

- Explore: He journals: *"When did I start believing I had to perform to be loved?"* He traces the script to a parent who only showed affection during wins, and a church culture that affirmed performance more than presence.

- Innovate: Jamal restructures his week. He intentionally sets time for slow, non-performing activities, walking, listening, resting, with no end goal except presence. He challenges himself to be known without showcasing success.

- Navigate: He redefines success: not applause, but alignment. Not spotlight, but substance. He tells himself, *"I want to live loved, not liked."* He writes out a new value statement rooted in authenticity and intimacy.

- Activate: Jamal meets with a mentor, not to report achievements, but to tell the truth. He confesses, *"I'm tired of being impressive. I want to be whole."* He begins practicing affirmations that remind him his worth is not earned, it's inherent.

Leon (The Victim)

Saboteur Lens: Leon grew up being overlooked. Now, even in leadership, he withdraws emotionally when he feels misunderstood. He longs for affirmation but doesn't know how to ask. He often spirals into self-pity and assumes no one truly sees his heart.

Sage Reframe:

- Empathize: Leon takes a breath and acknowledges the younger version of himself who was never seen or celebrated. He gently speaks to that child within, "You deserved to be noticed. You are not invisible now."

- Explore: He gets curious: *What is this moment trying to teach me about my need to be validated?"* He remembers the patterns, childhood neglect, emotionally unavailable mentors, and names how they formed his withdrawal reflex.

- Innovate: Instead of withdrawing, Leon decides to communicate differently. He drafts a text to a trusted brother, saying, "Today I felt unseen, and I didn't want to say anything. But I need to talk." He's learning to ask, not hope.

- Navigate: Leon returns to his values. He writes in his journal, *"My value doesn't disappear when I'm overlooked. I will live as someone already seen by God."* He recites Psalm 139: "You have searched me, Lord, and you know me."

- Activate: Leon joins a prayer group not to lead, but to be honest. He shares his fear of invisibility and lets the room hold his story. For the first time in a while, he feels known, and not just noticed.

Quincy (The Hyper-Rational)

Saboteur Lens: Quincy leads with logic and scripture but avoids emotional conversations. When his wife cries, he shuts down or quotes Bible verses instead of offering comfort. Emotions feel unsafe, so he intellectualizes every problem, even his pain.

Sage Reframe:

- Empathize: Quincy recognizes that logic became his armor growing up in a home where emotions were ignored or punished. He gently acknowledges, *"It wasn't safe to feel then, but it's safe to feel now."*

- Explore: He asks himself, *"What am I protecting myself from by avoiding feelings?"* He remembers how emotion was seen as weakness in his upbringing and ministry context.

- Innovate: Quincy writes down alternative ways he could respond when his wife shares emotion: "I'm here for you," "That sounds painful," or simply sitting with her in silence. He begins to practice emotional fluency, just like he once studied Greek and Hebrew.

- Navigate: He reflects on his values, intimacy, presence, truth. He writes in his journal, *"If I want to be fully present with those I love, I have to learn to feel, not just fix."*

- Activate: The next time his wife begins to cry, he stays. He doesn't quote scripture, he offers his presence. It's uncomfortable, but it's holy. And afterward, he realizes: connection doesn't require control.

Darius (The Hyper-Vigilant)

Saboteur Lens: Darius constantly scans for threats, criticism, betrayal, or failure. Growing up in tough neighborhoods and hostile churches taught him to stay on edge. Even in moments of peace, he expects the worst, living in quiet anxiety.

Sage Reframe:

- Empathize: Darius acknowledges that hyper-vigilance helped him survive environments where danger was real. He reminds his younger self, *"You did what you had to do to feel safe. But now, you are not in that same warzone."*

- Explore: He asks, *"What am I afraid will happen if I let my guard down?"* This reflection leads him to see how he's brought the trauma of his past into safe spaces, punishing the present for the pain of yesterday.

- Innovate: He imagines a world where not everyone is a threat. Darius begins crafting new ways to engage relationships, starting small, like trusting someone with a minor task and celebrating how it doesn't end in disaster.

- Navigate: Reconnecting to his values of peace, leadership, and stability, he writes: *"I want to build trust, not walls. I want to respond with wisdom, not react from fear."*

- Activate: Darius begins practicing breathwork and mindfulness before meetings. When anxiety rises, he pauses, grounds himself, and chooses faith over fear, even if just for the next 5 minutes. Over time, his nervous system learns that safety isn't weakness. It's worship.

Chris (The Restless)

Saboteur Lens: Chris can't sit still. He's always launching something, another podcast, another program, another service. When asked to rest, he deflects. Productivity keeps him from facing deeper issues he's not ready to name.

Sage Reframe:

- Empathize: Chris reflects on the early seasons of his life when stillness meant stagnation. He acknowledges the boy who felt forgotten unless he was doing something. The Sage whispers, *"You are not your output. You are not invisible. You are already seen."*

- Explore: Instead of rushing into his next idea, Chris pauses and asks, *"What am I running from?"* He journals about the silence that scares him and begins to notice a pattern of fleeing discomfort.

- Innovate: Chris dreams up a new rhythm, weekly moments of tech-free silence. He designs creative sabbath spaces: walking without headphones, praying without preaching, building without branding. He leans into the discomfort to find new peace.

- Navigate: Anchored in his value for depth, not just breadth, he sets a new internal GPS: *"I'd rather grow roots than just bear fruit. I want to be present, not just productive."*

- Activate: Chris takes a brave step, he says no to a new speaking engagement. Instead, he spends that weekend in stillness with a close friend, letting silence speak. For the first time in years, he rests without guilt.

Terrence (The Avoider)

Saboteur Lens: Terrence knows his church is toxic, but he won't confront the dysfunction. He avoids hard conversations with his team and pacifies conflict with over-spiritualization. Avoidance has kept the peace, but it's killing his passion.

Sage Reframe:

- Empathize: Terrence honors the younger version of himself who learned early on that speaking up invited danger. The Sage reminds him, *"You did what you needed to survive, but you don't have to lead from fear anymore."*

- Explore: He becomes curious about what's really holding him back. Is it fear of rejection? A memory of being dismissed? The Sage helps him name his fear without shame and trace its root.

- Innovate: Instead of issuing ultimatums or continuing silence, Terrence drafts a team covenant, one grounded in grace, truth, and accountability. He imagines a church culture where honesty and healing can co-exist.

- Navigate: With values like integrity, stewardship, and wellness guiding him, Terrence prayerfully plans a courageous conversation with his leadership team, one that opens the door to change, not chaos.

- Activate: He initiates the conversation. Not with aggression, but with clarity. He names what's been unsaid, sets healthy boundaries, and begins dismantling dysfunction with grace.

When we let the Sage speak, the story shifts. Not because pain disappears, but because we stop partnering with the lie and start building with truth.

Sidebar: Saboteur vs. Sage – Rewriting the Response

Situation	Saboteur Response	Sage Response
You make a mistake	"You always mess up." (Judge)	"What can I learn from this?" (Explore)
A project goes off track	"Fix it yourself." (Controller)	"Who can help me move forward?" (Navigate)
You feel emotionally overwhelmed	"Push through, ignore it." (Avoider)	"Let's feel and process this." (Empathize)
You feel invisible	"No one cares." (Victim)	"I am still worthy and called." (Activate)

Every time we choose empathy over judgment, vision over fear, and truth over trauma, we let the Sage lead.

Reflection Questions

- Think of a season when you stayed busy to avoid feeling hurt or inadequate. What were you trying to prove, and to whom?

  _____

  _____

  _____

  _____

  _____

- Looking at the Hustle vs. Holy chart, which lie has been loudest in your life? (*e.g., "If I stop, I'll fall behind" or "If I'm not achieving, I'm not worthy"*)

  _____

  _____

  _____

  _____

  _____

- Be honest: what has hustling while hurting cost you in terms of joy, intimacy, health, or connection with God?

  _____

  _____

  _____

_____

_____

- Among the examples of Marcus, Devon, Omar, Anthony, Jamal, Leon, Quincy, Darius, Chris, and Terrence, whose story felt most like yours? Why?

_____

_____

_____

_____

_____

- What Sage power do you need to practice right now: Empathize, Explore, Innovate, Navigate, or Activate? What's one small step you can take to activate it?

_____

_____

_____

_____

_____

- If you fully believed your worth wasn't tied to your work, what would you stop doing? What would you start doing?

_____

_____

_____

_____

_____

- Reflect on Matthew 11:28: *"Come to me, all who are weary and burdened, and I will give you rest."* What does it look like for you to actually come and rest?

_____

_____

_____

_____

_____

Scripture Meditation

Matthew 11:28

"Come to me, all who are weary and burdened, and I will give you rest."

Prayer:

"God, I'm tired of grinding for worth. Help me unlearn the lie that hustle is holy. Remind me that I am your beloved, even when I'm still. Teach me how to live from identity, not for it. Give me courage to rest, to trust, and to rebuild on a healed foundation. Amen."

CHAPTER 6

I'M WORKING ON ME – BREAKING THE HABIT OF HURTING MYSELF

Sometimes the greatest enemy to your next level isn't out there, it's in you. Not the devil. Not your haters. Not your past. But the part of you that's been conditioned to believe you don't deserve healing. The part of you that's been trained to expect rejection. The part of you that calls failure "familiar" and fear "wisdom." Many of us block our own becoming, not because we're weak, but because we've spent years surviving in dysfunction. And when survival becomes your identity, wholeness can feel like a threat.

We're digging into the lies we've rehearsed, the habits we've normalized, and the fears we've mistaken for discernment. We'll call it out, confess it fully, and start carving a new way forward.

Why Dig?

Before a man can rebuild, he must first be willing to dig. To excavate. To confront not only what has been built on shaky ground, but also to acknowledge what's still buried beneath it. That's what this chapter is about, not just looking at what we've done, but uncovering the deeper reasons why we've done it.

This chapter is the next step in the journey. Not just confronting sabotage, but committing to stop participating in your own pain.

"God, give us the strength to be stronger than our saboteurs so that we stop the sin of self-sabotage.", Opening prayer, I'm Working on Me Session Two

Self-Sabotage Is a Sin of Agreement

Self-sabotage is more than poor habits, it's misplaced agreements. Somewhere along the way, we agreed to shrink. We agreed to settle. We agreed to be less than who God made us.

But those agreements can be broken. And that's what this chapter is about:

- Identifying the old vows
- Replacing survival tactics with spiritual truth
- Reclaiming agency over our own healing

Essentially this is the beginning of reformation. Somehow we were formed to believe we weren't deserving of the best GOD has for us. Somehow we bought into the lie that as Black Men we were double cursed, cursed by Adam's sin and cursed by Ham's mistake, and so we have adopted a problem where we cancel ourselves out of our promise before we even show up. We don't even know our full potential, for our saboteurs are constantly self-talking us out of even trying.

The Cycles We Repeat

I once posed a difficult question to a group of Black male clergy: "What are the behaviors that once worked for you but are now blocking your growth?" The room was quiet for a moment, and then the floodgates opened. Leaders began naming patterns that once protected them but now prevent progress. Some confessed that procrastination, once a shield from failure, had morphed into a cage of perfectionism. Others admitted that people-pleasing, once mistaken for pastoral care, had become a prison of codependence. Many recognized that their tendency to over-function

96

was actually a way to avoid emotional vulnerability. Some realized that what they had labeled as introversion was in fact isolation, self-protection dressed in spiritual language.

Every one of those behaviors started as a survival tool. But they've become sabotage scripts.

At some point in their lives those behaviors benefitted them, and as a result they began relying on the behavior. It allowed them to survive a specific situation, but it became their standard operating procedure. The saboteur voices became their sole source of inspiration and it hindered and even hurt them.

Digging Deeper: The Work Begins

Let me take you back to a moment that marked the beginning of my excavation. I had just come out of a season of intense shame. My marriage was bruised. My ministry was shaken. My soul was tender. And I realized I didn't really know the man I saw in the mirror. I had been operating under layers, titles, trauma, triumphs, and trials, but none of those were the truest me.

So I asked myself a hard question: *Who am I beyond the pain, beyond the platform, beyond the performance?*

And then I began to work. Not the kind of work you do with a mic or a meeting agenda, but the soul work. The therapy work. The spiritual excavation that required silence, honesty, and the willingness to sit in the dirt of my decisions. It is the work of renovation, of deconstruction for the purpose of reforming, reinventing, and reimagining the possibility of the person.

Let me first say that you reading this book, no matter where your life has been or is now, you have possibility. You have purpose, and the evidence is in the fact that in order to read this book you must be breathing. Your breath is all the evidence you need that GOD loves you. What do I mean? Well have you had to at once pause and tell yourself to breathe? Have you had to make sure that before your last breath ran out that your next breath was taken? NO,

GOD loves you so much that your breath is in GOD's control, so if GOD is controlling it, and you are still breathing, then GOD still has plans for you and your life.

Once you realize that, you should simultaneously realize the value of your life…the worth of your life. GOD loves you enough and values you enough to take personal care of your breathing, so that you can concentrate on everything else. Now you must steward your breath. You must decide that your breath is valuable enough, that the Gift GOD gave you of breathing is so special that you make the stewardship of it sacred. Right now… this isn't about the past and can't be retroactively applied, but right now and moving forward, let's make the decision… the choice… to move forward and be reformed!!

Biblical Evidence of Self-Image Reformation

Moses had to confront his insecurities before he could lead Israel (Exodus 4). Even though God appeared to him in a burning bush and called him directly, Moses still argued: *"Who am I that I should go to Pharaoh?"* and *"I am slow of speech and tongue."* He didn't just walk into leadership overnight, he had to face the internalized shame of his past, his failures in Egypt, and his fear of inadequacy. The self-work for Moses meant trusting that God's presence was enough to cover his perceived lack.

Elijah had to recover and reset before he could hear God again (1 Kings 19). After his greatest public victory over the prophets of Baal, he fell into deep despair and even asked God to take his life. The mighty prophet collapsed under exhaustion, fear, and loneliness. God didn't send him back to work right away, instead, He let Elijah sleep, eat, and regain his strength before gently revealing Himself in a still, small voice. The self-work for Elijah meant learning that his value wasn't tied to his dramatic victories, but to his belovedness and God's quiet presence.

Peter had to be restored from shame before stepping fully into his purpose (John 21). After denying Jesus three times, Peter returned to fishing, to the life he knew before his call. He was haunted by his failure. But Jesus met him on the shore, cooked him breakfast, and asked him three times, *"Do you love me?"*, once for each denial, and then re-commissioned him: *"Feed my sheep."* The self-work for Peter meant forgiving himself and believing that his failure didn't disqualify him from his calling.

Even Paul admitted his own inner battle, saying: *"I don't do what I want to do, but I do the very thing I hate"* (Romans 7:15). The great apostle didn't shy away from confessing his struggle with sin and his divided heart. He acknowledged his ongoing need for grace and transformation. The self-work for Paul meant living in the tension between his humanity and God's sanctifying power, and pressing on anyway.

This is holy work.

This is necessary work.

God's calling doesn't bypass the heart, it meets you there.

And this kind of wrestling, resting, and reimagining didn't just happen in the Bible. It wasn't just the work of Biblical characters to do, no it is the work of all of us who have been created by GOD. We must work to become our best self, and we must know it still happens in us.

Mirror Moment – A Word from Otis Moss III

In his book *Dancing in the Darkness*, Otis Moss III speaks to the sacred work of confronting our shadowed selves:

> "There is no healing without honesty, and no trans-
> formation without truth. You must be willing to dance
> with your darkness to discover your divine."

That line wrecked me. Because for so long, I avoided the dance, I just wanted deliverance. I didn't want to sit in the silence with my shadow. But the darkness wasn't meant to destroy me, it was where God was inviting me to wrestle. As Jacob wrestled all night with

GOD to not be blessed and have his name changed, but also to come to terms with who he was, with who he had become, with the weight of the image he presented to GOD, but not the image GOD would allow him to be content with.

This too is working on me. Sitting with the discomfort. Naming the grief. Being honest about what hurts, so that healing can finally begin.

Moss goes on to talk about the transformation that comes from mirror work.

"Transformation from victim to hero is not something you accomplish in private. The heroic transformations that I'm talking about happen not alone but through our relationship. I think of Deacon Lawerence Miles, twenty years sober as I write this, who once struggled with alcoholism. His disease came between him and his children because he was too drunk or too focused on getting his next drink to show up for them. One day his daughter was in the hospital and he tried to pull himself together to visit her. She was the one who was sick, but when he got to the hospital room he was drunk, weeping and crying so much that finally he had to find a bathroom where he could pull himself together. He tells the story of how he reached for a paper towel, and in the reflection of the metal towel dispenser, he saw his own face. The image was warped and misshapen in the uneven metal, but he could make out his bloodshot teary eyes, the wet mess from his nose, and he felt, "My GOD, that's who I am? That misshapen thing is my soul. I never want to see myself that way again. That's not who my daughter needs." Deacon Miles promised himself then that he would remember that moment. He would no longer be defined to the world as the disappointment who did what the bottle told him to do. He would become the hero he was called to be. A reliable father for his children. Of course, one moment of resolution does not change anyone. There was hard work to be done. Deacon Miles went into a rehab program, got sober, and now sees a very different man in the bathroom mirror. In part because he has never forgotten the misshapen image he saw that day. This is a heroic choice.

As poet, Mary Oliver, writes in her poem, *The Journey*! "One day you finally knew what you had to do and began. Though the voices around you kept shouting their bad advice. Though the whole house began to tremble and you felt the old tug at your ankles, 'Mend my life!' each voice cried, but you didn't stop. You knew what you had to do. Though the wind pried with its stiff fingers at the very foundations. Though their melancholy was terrible, it was already late enough and a wild night and the road full of fallen branches and stones. But little by little as you left their voices behind, the stars began to burn through the sheets of clouds and there was a new voice which you slowly recognized as your own that kept you company as you strolled deeper and deeper into the world determined to do the only thing you could do. Determined to save the only life you could save."

My Mirror Moment: When I Believed God Was Punishing Me

For a long time, I believed that my daughter's death was God's way of punishing me.

When Noelle died in that car accident, something inside me shattered. She was my little girl, my light. But instead of grieving as a father, I grieved as a man full of shame.

I told myself her death was my fault. That it was God's way of paying me back for all the ways I'd failed. For all the indiscretions. For all the lies. For cheating on my wife.

And every night, I would lay next to, Karen, my wife, the woman I'd betrayed, and wonder if she was silently blaming me too. I'd lie there in the dark, feeling the weight of her grief and assuming it was aimed at me. Even when she never said it, I carried the belief that our daughter died because of me.

That shame was a heavy, silent companion. It told me I didn't deserve comfort. That I didn't deserve to heal. That I needed to carry this guilt as penance.

But slowly, painfully, God began to untangle that lie. Through prayer. Through tears. Through counseling. Through quiet moments when He reminded me of His heart.

One day as I was in the bathroom, face wet with tears, I heard Him say, in a way only my soul could hear: *"I don't punish like that. Noelle's life and her death were not a transaction. They were part of My will, not My wrath."*

It didn't all change overnight. But little by little, I began to forgive myself. I began to see that her death wasn't about persuading me to do right. It wasn't about punishing me for my wrongs.

It was tragic, yes. But it was not my fault.

It was her time, and somehow, even in that, God was still good.

And I had to stop punishing myself for a punishment God never gave me.

Now, when I think of Noelle, I still feel the ache, but I also feel the love. I remember her as my daughter, not as my consequence.

And I trust that she's with Him, whole and waiting, and that even in this, His grace has been enough for me too.

The Assignment: Internal Inventory

I challenge you in the middle of this chapter to do some immediate work. Some "Mirror Work" of your own. Let's take some time and really reflect on who you see, who you see at your worst moments, who you want to see, and who GOD wants you to see. Those could potentially be four different images.

> "Journal your sabotage. Don't wait until it explodes, catch it in the act."

Try this reflection each night:

1. What did I do today that worked against my peace?

2. What thought was behind that action?

3. What truth could I have spoken over myself instead?

This is not just therapy, it's theology. Romans 12:2 calls it "renewing the mind."

From Saboteur to Sage (Continued) Revisit your saboteurs from Chapter 4. Now ask:

- What triggers them?

- Who reinforces them?

- How do they speak when you're close to breakthrough?

Then call in your Sage (The work we just did in Chapter 5):

- Empathy for your younger self

- Curiosity about the pain

- Courage to respond differently

SideBar: SAGE vs. SABOTEUR – A Response Chart (let's put this as a chart)

When I Sabotage...	When I Choose the Sage...
I isolate	I reach out for help
I perform for love	I practice being present in love
I numb my emotions	I name and feel my emotions
I replay my shame	I rewrite my story with grace
I strive to be seen	I remember I'm already known by GOD

Working on Me Means…

- Choosing growth over guilt

- Choosing self-awareness over self-protection

- Choosing accountability over image
- Choosing God's truth over trauma's voice

Reflection Questions:

- What's one sabotage behavior you're finally ready to stop calling "normal"?

_____

_____

_____

_____

_____

- Who have you hurt because you didn't confront your pain?

_____

_____

_____

_____

_____

- What do you believe God is waiting to do _through you_ once you stop sabotaging _you_?

_____

_____

_____

_____

_____

- When you look in the "mirror", in your worst moments, what do you actually see? And how does that image differ from how God sees you?

_____

_____

_____

_____

_____

- Which old agreements or vows (spoken or unspoken) have you been living by that no longer serve you, and what would it take to break them?

_____

_____

_____

_____

_____

- What survival habits have quietly become sabotage, and what new habits could you begin practicing instead?

_____

_____

_____

_____

_____

- When have you mistaken fear for wisdom or called dysfunction "normal" because it felt familiar? What would
  choosing faith over fear look like today?

  _____

  _____

  _____

  _____

  _____

- Who in your life needs you to do this inner work, not just
  for you, but so you can show up whole for them?

  _____

  _____

  _____

  _____

  _____

Scripture Meditation
Romans 12:2
"Be transformed by the renewing of your mind."

Prayer:

"God, I am working on me. Not for applause. Not for performance. But because I'm tired of bleeding in cycles I was called to break. Show me where I've agreed with lies. Help me become a safe space, for myself and others. Make me whole. Make me new. Amen."

CHAPTER 7

MESSY MATURITY, COMING TO YOURSELF IN THE PIGPEN

There are moments when clarity doesn't arrive in the sanctuary, but in the mud. Not at the altar, but in the aftermath. Not with applause, but with the aching awareness that something has to change.

Luke 15:17 says:

> *"But when he came to himself…"*

That simple phrase captures a profound truth: at some point, we all have to come to ourselves. And for many of us, that realization doesn't come wrapped in grace and glitter, it comes dressed in grit and grime.

The pigpen is where messy maturity happens. It's where you discover the difference between just growing older and truly growing up. Because here's the reality: maturity has nothing to do with age. Biology makes you male or female, but maturity makes you a man or a woman.

As 1 Corinthians 13:11 says: *"When I was a child, I spoke as a child, I thought as a child, I reasoned like a child. But when I became…"* And that's the hard part, the becoming.

Some people seem to glide through life gracefully, learning lessons in classrooms or at their parents' feet. But others of us, we have to touch the stove. We have to get burned. We have to walk through valleys, be swallowed by fish, sit in pigpens.

This chapter is for those who had to go through some stuff. For those who ignored all the signs, who thought they could skip the process, who demanded blessings they weren't ready to carry. For those who found out the hard way that some lessons only come through the mud.

And here's the main idea:

> *While some people have the privilege of graceful maturation, some of us receive our greatest life lessons out of our messiest situations.*

That's where we find ourselves in the story, with a young man, born into privilege, who asked for his inheritance early, squandered it on what he thought was freedom, and ended up broke, hungry, and feeding pigs. And then, right there, surrounded by slop, he came to himself.

In the middle of his mess, the light bulb came on. And I want you to know: there is nothing wrong with being a late bloomer. Even if you had to learn the hard way, even if you didn't listen the first (or fifth) time, even if it took longer than you thought, it's never too late to come to yourself.

The Prodigal's Mirror Moment

The young man in Luke 15 had everything: a name, a house, an inheritance. But one day he got restless. He confused his birthright with readiness, mistaking access for maturity and ownership for identity.

So he did what many of us have done, he made an arrogant ask. He essentially told his father: "I can do better without you. Give me what's mine." Maybe you've been there too, believing you could handle more than you were actually ready for. Maybe you thought leaving would make you free, not realizing it would only leave you empty.

And so he left, full of money but hollow in purpose. He chased applause, pleasure, and autonomy. He went to a far-off country where no one knew his name, where he could act grown without being reminded of who he really was.

But then came the famine.

The money dried up.

The friends disappeared.

And there he was, in a pigpen, feeding what he once found unclean, craving what could never satisfy.

Have you been there? Sitting in a place you swore you'd never end up? Looking around at the mess and wondering how you got so far from home?

One day, in the middle of his mess, something shifted. He realized his experience didn't match his expectation. What he thought would feel like freedom now felt like failure. And his pride, which had kept him from turning back sooner, was finally broken by hunger and humiliation.

And then the miracle happened:

"But when he came to himself…"

He didn't come to himself because the conditions improved, he came to himself because the illusion finally shattered.

Sometimes it takes the mud to make the mirror clear.

And maybe that's where you are now, finally ready to come to yourself.

Four Questions for Messy Maturity

The pigpen doesn't just happen overnight. Neither does the journey out of it. But if you're willing to be honest with yourself, you'll discover that the mess has been trying to teach you something all along. Here are four questions to help you uncover what went wrong, what broke, and how to rebuild.

What got me in the mess?

We rarely stumble into the pigpen by accident. Usually, there are patterns, choices, and attitudes that paved the way.

- An Arrogant Ask, Like the prodigal, sometimes we demand blessings before we're mature enough to handle them. We think we're ready for responsibilities, relationships, or recognition, but we're still growing, and it shows.

- Experience Didn't Match Expectation, We assumed life away from accountability would feel free and full, but it turned out hollow and heavy. The dream we chased wasn't what we thought it would be.

- Pride Made the Problem Worse, Even when the warning signs came, we didn't turn back. We dug in our heels, convincing ourselves we could fix it, until we sank deeper.

Be honest: Which of these patterns do you recognize in your story? What choices led you here? Naming them is the first step to changing them.

What happened in the mess?

The pigpen is more than just a place, it's a teacher. And its lessons can hurt.

- Missing Moments, In your pursuit of something else, you missed out on what really mattered. Birthdays, friendships, peace of mind, all slipped through your fingers while you were distracted by the wrong things.

- Devaluing Yourself, At some point, you started to believe the lie that your mess defined you. You looked around and decided, I'm not worthy of more. This is who I am now.

- Mistaking Failure for Future, The longer you stayed in the slop, the more you began to think it was your permanent address. You forgot that grace still had your name on it.

Pause here and ask yourself: What did the mess reveal about you? What did it take from you? But also, what did it teach you?

What steps do I take to come out of my mess?

You don't wake up one morning magically whole again. Coming out of the pigpen is a series of intentional steps, small but courageous.

- I Make Up My Mind, My Mess is Not My Most

  You choose to believe, even in your lowest place, that this is not the best God has for you. That your identity is greater than your condition.

- I Remove Myself From What I Made My Reality

  You take the hard step of leaving what you've been calling "home," even if it's uncomfortable and uncertain.

- I Risk Everything to Return as Reformed

  You walk back toward wholeness, not as who you were when you left, but as someone who has grown through the dirt.

These steps don't happen perfectly. You might feel afraid, ashamed, even unworthy, but you take them anyway. Because the walk home is worth it.

What happened when I matured out of my mess?

The beauty of messy maturity is that it doesn't just change your circumstances, it changes your perspective.

- Who I Worried About Was Waiting on Me, You thought no one would take you back, but the Father was watching, waiting, ready to meet you on the road.

- Though I Caused the Offense, I Couldn't Control the Outcome, You rehearsed your apology, expecting punishment, but you were met with grace.

- Dysfunction Was Never Meant to Be My Destiny, The robe, the ring, the feast reminded you: You were always a child of the house. Your mess didn't erase your identity.

When you finally come to yourself and start the journey home, you find what was true all along: you were never disqualified. You were just waiting to wake up to it.

What Maturity Looks Like

Maturity in messy places is never glamorous. It starts small, quiet, and honest:

- Making up your mind that your mess is not your most, that this is not the best God has for you.

- Removing yourself from what you had made your reality, even if it feels risky.

- Risking everything to return home reformed, dirty but determined.

Messy Maturity: My Pigpen Moment

For years, I thought being a Black man meant proving myself in all the wrong ways.

I believed my manhood was measured by how many women I could entertain, keeping my wife from ever getting too comfortable, always making sure she knew I had options. That was my twisted definition of strength: control, conquest, and keeping her on edge.

As a young preacher, I thought my worth came from what I wore and where I was seen. Custom suits, fancy shoes, expensive colognes, I thought those things made me somebody. I thought every flyer with my face on it, every invitation to preach, every big platform validated me.

And for a while, it worked, at least, it felt like it did. Those moments gave me a rush, a sense of significance, a temporary high.

But then came my pigpen moment, the moment I looked around at my life and realized: all of it, the women, the platforms, the applause, the suits, had given me sensations, but not peace. Moments, but not joy.

I had sacrificed time with my family for stages full of strangers. I had traded the love of my wife for the illusion of being desired.

It hit me one day, like the prodigal son among the husks and mud: I had been chasing validation and neglecting the very things that truly matter.

That was the moment I decided to come home. To myself. To my wife. To my family. To God.

Because nothing, no platform, no applause, no possession, can compare to real peace and real love.

Signs You are Maturing out of Your Mess

- You own your reality and choose growth despite the mess.
- You stop blaming and start reflecting.
- You let failure teach you without letting it define you.
- You seek healing over applause.
- You choose integrity over image.
- You embrace growth even when it's awkward or lonely.
- You admit the pigpen is beneath you, but also necessary, because it brought you back to yourself.

Reflection Questions

- Where was your pigpen moment? What brought you to yourself?

_____

_____

_____

_____

_____

- What illusions had to break before you could begin healing?

_____

_____

_____

_____

_____

- What does "coming home" look like in your life right now?

_____

_____

_____

_____

_____

- Who have you hurt while trying to prove you were fine?

_____

_____

_____

_____

_____

- What is God saying to the real you?

_____

_____

_____

_____

_____

Scripture Meditation
Luke 15:17
"But when he came to himself, he said, 'How many of my father's hired servants have bread enough and to spare, and I perish with hunger!'"

Prayer

God, I'm coming to myself. I'm tired of pretending, tired of performing, tired of the pigpen. Thank You for not giving up on me. Even in my dirt, You see me as Yours. Help me walk back to You without shame but with expectation. Heal me on the way. Love me through the layers. And remind me that home is still mine. Amen.

SECTION TWO SUMMARY

FROM WOUNDS TO WISDOM, HEALING THE MAN WITHIN

Section Two was about more than self-awareness, it was about self-confrontation and self-compassion. It invited us into the courageous work of healing the man beneath the mask.

We named the lies.

We challenged the hustle.

We confronted the sabotage.

We stood in the pigpen and chose to come home.

In Chapter 4, *Sabotage Scripts, When the Lies Sound Like Truth*, we uncovered the hidden narratives running in the background of our lives, lies we've memorized from fathers, coaches, culture, and even the church. We learned to identify, trace, and rewrite those scripts with God's truth, understanding that the gospel meets us in the middle of our lie and walks us toward the light.

In Chapter 5, *Unlearning Survival, The Cost of Hustling While Hurting*, we exposed the hustle for what it really is: a mask. We wrestled with the dangerous idea that productivity equals worth, and we reclaimed rest as holy and identity as rooted in being, not doing. We dared to believe that our value is not tied to applause or performance, but anchored in God's love.

In Chapter 6, *I'm Working on Me, Breaking the Habit of Hurting Myself*, we got honest about the ways we participate in our own pain. We dug beneath the surface to identify the misplaced agreements and sabotaging habits that once helped us survive but now keep us stuck. We began the sacred excavation, confronting what's buried and choosing to rewrite the vows that no longer serve us.

In Chapter 7, *Messy Maturity, Coming to Yourself in the Pigpen*, we stood in the mud and admitted that the mess has been teaching us all along. We embraced the truth that sometimes you have to fail to finally grow up. We owned our choices, broke our illusions, and discovered that even in the pigpen, God was waiting, ready to clothe us in grace and call us home.

This section was not about arriving.

It was about awakening.

It was about realizing that survival is not enough, that the lies are not our truth, that the hustle is not our identity, and that the pigpen is not our home.

You've begun to confront the man you've become so you can step into the man you were created to be.

Now, we move forward, toward restoration, wholeness, and wisdom lived out loud.

Let's keep building.

SECTION THREE

WHO I REALLY AM, RECLAIMING AND REFORMING THE TRUTH OF MY IDENTITY

There is no healing without identity. No transformation without truth. And no wholeness without first understanding who you really are, not who you've performed to be, not who others mistook you to be, but who GOD created you to be from the very beginning.

This section is the heartbeat of identity reformation. It is the moment in the journey when we stop rehearsing the wounds and begin to reclaim the truth. It's about going back to the origin story, not just of your pain, but of your purpose. Drawing from the foundation laid across seven biblically-based identity re-formation sessions, this section becomes the theological and psychological reset.

This begins the real "Mirror Work." When you look in the mirror, who do you see? Do you like who you see? Are you comfortable with who you see? Is who you see who you really want to be? Is who you see who GOD created? Perhaps the better question is: Is GOD pleased with the you GOD sees? If you were to look through GOD's eyes, would GOD see the person HE created?

If the answer is, "No," don't be hard on yourself. Oftentimes we become who others say we are or who we feel we need to be to seek the approval of people, circumstances, or even systems. But when you become anyone other than who GOD created, you've made the things you became into gods.

Mirror Moment:

Ask yourself: *"Who am I trying to impress?" "Who gave me this definition of success?" "Do I want to be healed or just liked?"*

This becoming is often rooted in your formation. And the only way to heal that is through reformation. Don't let age or how long you've been "this way" discourage you. Like hardened pottery, you can be refired in the kiln, reheated in the fire of transformation, and made malleable again. You can be reshaped. And that work begins now.

We begin with your identity.

Dr. Howard Thurman, mystic theologian and mentor to Dr. King, once told graduating women at Spelman College in 1980:

> "There is something in every one of you that waits, listens for the genuine in yourself, and if you cannot hear it, you will never find whatever it is for which you are searching. And if you hear it and do not follow it, it was better that you had never been born. You are the only you that has ever lived; your idiom is the only idiom of its kind… and if you cannot hear the sound of the genuine in you, you will all your life spend your days on the ends of strings that somebody else pulls."

He continued:

> "There is something that waits and listens for the sound of the genuine in yourself. And sometimes, there is so much traffic in your mind, so many signals, so many impulses inherited through generations, long before you were even thought of in the mind of creation, and in the midst of all that noise, you've got to find out what your name is. Who are you? How does the sound of the genuine come through to you? … That sound is flowing through you."

In the chapters ahead, we will quiet the noise. We will cut the strings others pull. We will tune our ears to the sound of the genuine, and rediscover the truth of who we are. These chapters are for your mirror work, so they will be less about me and my story, but more about you realizing and rewriting your own story! Reforming your Reality.

Let's begin by looking at some truths about your identity.

CHAPTER 8

RELEARNING AND REMEMBERING WHO I AM, CONTEXT FROM CREATION

TEXT: Genesis 1:26-28

Before we can reclaim and reform our identity, we must start at the beginning, at our origin story. Who we really are is not defined by wounds, titles, achievements, or mistakes, but by the Creator's original intention. To remember and relearn ourselves, we return to Genesis, the book of beginnings, which tells not only the story of the world's creation but of your creation too.

This chapter is for those of us who ever felt our existence was accidental. This chapter is the counter to the crowd, whether it be family, or enemies, or even those saboteuring conversation partners in our head, that say we are a mistake, we have no purpose, and we are unwanted. This chapter is especially for us who take unnecessary risks believing our lives are trivial and meaningless. GOD's story of our existence is the perfect way to prove those of us who think and behave that way wrong.

Genesis was written to help a wandering, wounded people remember who they were and whose they were. Likely compiled and finalized during or after the Babylonian exile, it served as a theological declaration: *you are not random; you are not forgotten; you were made with meaning.* For people enslaved, displaced, and disoriented, Genesis proclaimed a truth they could stand on, and it still speaks that truth to you today.

Now, this text is about the beginning, but it wasn't written *in* the beginning. Moses, who is credited with writing the Books of Genesis, Exodus, Leviticus, Numbers, and Deuteronomy, wasn't there at creation. Through oral tradition, he heard the story of creation spoken over and over again, until one day he understood the need to record it.

Two key moments catalyzed this:

First, in Numbers 13–14, the spies returned from the Promised Land saying, "We seemed like grasshoppers in our own eyes." They forgot who they were. As punishment, they wandered the wilderness for forty years.

Second, in Numbers 20, Moses, frustrated with the people, struck the rock instead of speaking to it. Knowing he would not enter the Promised Land himself, he wrote down the stories so the next generation would not repeat the mistakes of the past.

You too have made enough mistakes. As you reform your identity, you must also remember who you truly are so you don't sabotage yourself again.

Genesis 1:26–28 opens our eyes to the first and most profound identity truth, *your existence is intentional.* You were thought about, planned, and fashioned with divine precision. The Creator said, *"Let Us make humankind in Our image, according to Our likeness…"* That declaration wasn't casual, it was calculated, deliberate, and full of grace. You are the crown of creation.

Mirror Moment:

Have I truly embraced the fact that I was made on purpose? Have I acknowledged that I carry the likeness of the Divine? Or have I been living as if my life was an afterthought?

Six Identity Truths to Embrace
You Were Consciously Created

Your existence was never accidental. Genesis 1:26 says: *"Then God said…"* That phrase, *God said,* in Hebrew implies more than mere speech. It means to **boldly proclaim**, to **speak with authority**, to **declare with intentionality**, even to **brag**.

So when the Creator was about to make you, there was a pause in the creative rhythm. A proclamation. A boastful declaration to the heavens and to creation: *"Wait until you see what I'm about to do next!"*

If you study the creation process carefully, you'll see the shift. From verse 3 of Genesis 1 to verse 25, the Creator spoke one thing after another into being: "Let there be light…" "Let the land produce…" "Let the waters swarm…" But when it came to *you,* the pattern changed. In verse 26, the Creator stops, consults within the divine self, and speaks aloud: *"Let Us make humankind in Our image…"*

Pause here: the Creator never paused to consult about light, land, or even the vast cosmos, but paused and deliberated before creating *you.*

What does this tell you?

It tells you that you are the pinnacle of the creation process. Everything created before you, light, land, sea, plants, animals, was good, but the Creator wanted something even greater. You were not just the next step in creation, you were the **crown of creation**.

That means you were **considered and contemplated before you were created**. You're not an accident. You're not a mistake. You're not a mishap. You are here on purpose.

Even if people told you otherwise, even if your parents didn't plan you, even if you've doubted your worth, know this: if you are breathing, you belong here. The fact that you exist means you were meant to exist.

You were *consciously created.*

Don't let anyone diminish your purpose. Don't let anyone convince you that you don't matter. Don't let anyone make you believe you are less than.

You're here because the Creator desired you to be here, and paused everything to imagine, proclaim, and craft you.

Mirror Work - You Were Consciously Created

Stand in front of the mirror, take a long look, and say aloud:

"I am not an accident. I am not an afterthought. Before I was formed, Heaven paused for me. The Creator declared me with joy and intention. I belong here because I was desired and designed."

Write down two lies you've believed about being unwanted or insignificant, and then write the truth next to them: *"I am here on purpose."*

You Were Created as Copies of the Creator

Not only were you **consciously created**, but you were also **created as a copy of the Creator**. Genesis 1:26 declares:

"Let Us make humankind in Our image, according to Our likeness, and let them have dominion..."

This one verse carries three profound truths about you: you reflect the Creator's **appearance**, embody the Creator's **attributes**, and exercise the Creator's **authority**.

Let's break that down:

You Reflect the Creator's Appearance

When you look in the mirror, you're not simply seeing flesh and bone, you are seeing a reflection of the Divine. You are evidence of beauty, dignity, and intentionality.

That truth alone should raise your self-esteem and ground your self-worth. Too often, we let others define how we see ourselves, comparing our looks to others, measuring ourselves against ideals in magazines, movies, or social media.

But here's a question: when was the last time you looked in the mirror and said, *"I look like my Creator"*?

From birth, many of us hear, *"You look just like your dad,"* or, *"You have your mother's eyes."* But rarely do we hear, *"You look like your Creator."*

What if instead of striving to look like someone else, someone on Instagram, someone at the office, someone on TV, you simply sought to reflect the image you were already made in?

When you recognize that you bear the Creator's image, you stop striving for someone else's approval and start walking in your inherent dignity.

You Embody the Creator's Attributes

The text goes further: *"according to Our likeness."* That speaks not just to appearance but to character, you embody the attributes of the Creator.

That means you carry creativity, compassion, justice, resilience, mercy, and love within you.

You have the creative brilliance that spoke galaxies into existence.

You have the mercy that forgives, even when it hurts.

You have the justice that speaks up for the voiceless.

You have the resilience that endures storms.

You have the love that heals wounds.

Your challenge is to cultivate those attributes and reflect them in the world, not just for yourself but for others.

You Exercise the Creator's Authority

Finally, the verse concludes: *"...and let them have dominion..."*

This is authority, not for domination, but for stewardship.

At the beginning of creation, when humans moved, the animals listened. When humans spoke, the earth responded. When humans appeared, the atmosphere shifted, because they carried the authority of the One who made them.

That authority still rests on you.

When you enter a room, you carry influence.

When you open your mouth, you can speak peace or stir chaos.

When you walk into spaces, you represent the One who sent you.

You are not just a participant in this world, you are an agent of change, a representative of the Creator. You are the Creator's **advertisement** (showing what goodness looks like), the Creator's **ambassador** (representing divine love even in hostile places), and the Creator's **activist** (pushing back against darkness and injustice wherever it shows up).

Mirror Work - You Were Created as Copies of the Creator

Look at yourself closely, really see yourself, and say:

"I reflect my Creator. My hands carry His creativity, my eyes hold His light, my voice echoes His justice and love. I walk in spaces with the dignity and authority of someone made in His image. I am not less than. I am a reflection of greatness."

List three ways you already embody the Creator's attributes, through your creativity, compassion, or strength, and commit to practicing them intentionally this week.

You Were Created Completely

This is one of the most powerful and freeing truths of your identity: you lack nothing essential. You were created *completely*.

Genesis 1:26 says:

"Then God said, 'Let Us make humankind in Our image...'", the word *make* here (Hebrew: **asah**) means to form or fashion out of something that already exists.

But then, in verse 27, it says:

"So God created humankind in His own image...", and here the word shifts to *created* (Hebrew: **bara**), which means to create something out of nothing, an act only the Creator can perform.

So what does that mean?

In verse 26, the Creator envisions you, shaping you from what already exists, but in verse 27, you are spoken into existence as a brand-new creation, complete from the beginning, with nothing missing.

Bara, Complete at Creation

The Hebrew concept of *bara* is significant because it implies that when the Creator creates, nothing further is required. When heaven and earth were *bara*, everything needed to sustain life was already embedded in creation.

When light was called forth, it didn't need to be created again, it was already present, waiting to be spoken into visibility.

When land appeared, it was already there beneath the water, waiting to be revealed.

When animals and plants reproduced, it was because their potential to multiply was already placed in them at creation.

And so it is with you.

Everything you need to fulfill your purpose is already inside you. You carry untapped potential waiting to be awakened. The dream is already seeded in you; it just needs to be cultivated.

The Rib and the Revelation

Even when humanity needed a partner, the Creator didn't create another being from scratch, but instead reached into Adam and drew out what was already there.

When the Creator fashioned the woman from Adam's rib, it was a declaration that nothing outside of you is required to make you whole, and even what you need for connection and partnership already exists within the design of humanity.

You don't have to compete for it.

You don't have to compare yourself to others.

You don't have to chase external validation.

You are already enough.

Call It Forth

Here's the catch: just because it's inside you doesn't mean it activates itself. You must speak it, believe it, and step into it.

If you want to be a healer, call forth the compassion and wisdom that's already in you.

If you want to lead, awaken the courage that's already there.

If you want to create, summon the vision that has been embedded in your soul from the start.

Too many of us are waiting for permission from others to activate what the Creator already placed in us. At your core, you are not broken, incomplete, or defective. Culture may try to convince you otherwise. Pain may try to persuade you that something's missing. But the Creator has already called you *very good*.

You don't need a title, a relationship, a degree, or a platform to be complete, you already are.

Mirror Work - You Were Created Completely

Take a deep breath and declare:

"I am not missing anything essential. I already have everything within me to fulfill my purpose. I don't need to compete, compare, or chase approval. The Creator has already given me all I need. I am already enough."

Write down one dormant dream, gift, or quality you've doubted in yourself, and then speak over it: "I call you forth. You are here. You are ready."

You Were Created to Be Community and Collaborative

Genesis 1:27 declares:

"…male and female God created them."

This truth goes beyond gender, it speaks to our design for **community**. You were never meant to walk through this life in isolation.

From the very beginning, the Creator embedded interdependence into creation. You were formed to thrive alongside others, not just to coexist, but to collaborate.

Even the Creator's own words in verse 26 reflect collaboration:

"Let us make humankind…"

From eternity, creation was birthed out of divine community, and you were made in that same communal image.

Why Community Matters

You were not designed to function as an island.

No single person can embody the fullness of the Creator's image on their own, but together, we reveal more of the divine.

Every person you encounter also carries the Creator's image, even if it is fractured or buried beneath hurt. Together, your gifts, perspectives, and presence weave a more complete picture of what the Creator intended.

As the sermon reminds us:

"No man is an island. Nobody can do it all by themselves. You were made because the attributes you have coincide with the attributes of others, and together, you create the fullness of what is needed for the community to flourish."

You Are Necessary

You matter. You are not replaceable or unnecessary.

Your unique gifts, voice, and presence fill a space in the world that no one else can occupy.

When you withhold yourself, you diminish the whole.

This is not about performance to gain approval, it is about understanding that your very existence contributes something essential to the community around you.

When you show up fully, bringing all of who you are, you empower others to do the same. When you hide yourself or diminish your gifts, you weaken the collective strength of the community.

Community is Collaboration, Not Competition

Community works when everyone brings their piece of the puzzle.

Your gifts aren't greater than anyone else's, but they are yours to offer.

When your gifts operate in harmony with others', the community grows, thrives, and reflects more of the Creator's glory.

But here's the key: your wholeness matters to the health of the whole.

If you neglect yourself, if you stay fractured and self-sabotaging, you cannot fully contribute to the community's flourishing.

Part of embracing your design for community is taking care of yourself so you can show up whole.

You were made to belong. You are a piece of this beautiful, divine puzzle, and no piece can replace you.

There is no **C-O-M-M-U-N-I-T-Y** without **U**.

Mirror Work - You Were Created to Be Community and Collaborative

Look at yourself and say:

"I was not made to walk alone. My presence enriches others, and theirs enrich mine. I carry something the world needs. I belong to the collective, and I am not replaceable."

Identify one way you've been isolating yourself and write down one step you can take to re-engage and offer your gifts to the community around you.

You Were Created for a Cause

At creation, you were not only *formed*, you were *assigned*.

You were not brought into being merely to exist, but to fulfill a specific purpose.

Genesis 1:26–28 reminds us:

"Let them have dominion… over the fish of the sea, over the birds of the air, over the cattle, over all the earth…"

And then verse 28 continues:

"Then God blessed them, and God said to them, 'Be fruitful and multiply; fill the earth and subdue it; have dominion…'"

There it is: a cause. A calling. A mission.

135

But notice what happens before the instructions are given, verse 28 begins with a blessing:

"God blessed them and said…"

Blessed Before You Were Tasked

You were **blessed before you were tasked**.

The blessing came *first*, before the assignment, before the productivity, before the dominion.

This means your worth is not measured by your work.

Your value is not dependent on what you produce.

Your cause flows out of your identity, not the other way around.

As the sermon beautifully says:

"You were sealed for success before you took a step. The blessing was not a reward for your labor, it was your inheritance from the beginning."

Placed with Purpose

You were placed in the right context for your gifts to meet the needs around you.

The community you exist in, your family, your vocation, your circle, has been designed as the field where your calling can grow.

But here is the warning:

Sometimes we chase places that were not meant for us, seeking validation where we don't belong.

When we plant ourselves in unassigned soil, we struggle to grow and bear fruit.

You will thrive where you were *placed*, not where you *please*.

Find the place that honors your gifts, that draws out your best, and where you can multiply the goodness you carry.

Productivity is Not About Possessions

"Be fruitful and multiply" does not simply mean acquiring material success or producing things to impress others.

It means **reproducing the divine image within you**, replicating your gifts, your character, your wisdom, your love, so others can flourish too.

Here's the sobering thought:

If you do not heal from your self-sabotaging patterns, you risk reproducing them in others.

When you are not conscious of your cause, you pass down pain instead of purpose.

You were created to reproduce wholeness, to multiply goodness, and to replicate the image of the One who made you, not to perpetuate brokenness.

You Are Equipped for Your Cause

GOD made sure to give you exactly what you need for what you're called to do.

You have the authority to steward creation, not to dominate, but to cultivate, protect, and care for it.

You have been equipped and empowered to handle what is yours.

Don't waste energy comparing your assignment to someone else's.

You have your own lane, your own field, your own cause.

You were created on purpose *for* a purpose.

Stop wandering through life wondering if you matter.

You matter because you carry a cause only you can fulfill.

And you were already blessed to succeed at it.

Mirror Work - You Were Created for a Cause

Stand confidently before the mirror and say:

"I was not just made to exist, I was made for a cause. I was blessed before I was tasked. My purpose flows from who I am, not from what I earn. My cause is mine to fulfill, and I am already equipped for it."

Write down what you believe your cause is, even if it's just a whisper of an idea, and one small action you will take this week to honor it.

You Were Created to Be Covered Continuously

This final truth in the creation narrative is perhaps the most comforting:

You were never sent out uncovered.

Genesis 1:28 says:

"Then God blessed them and said to them…"

Before the first instruction.

Before the first failure.

Before the first moment of doubt.

You were blessed, covered in divine approval, love, and care.

Covered Before You Contributed

The Hebrew word used for "blessed" in verse 28 is *barak*.

It means to kneel, to lay hands on, to speak words of affirmation, and to surround with favor.

It's the image of a loving parent placing their hands on a child's head, looking them in the eye, and saying:

"I see you. I'm proud of you. I'm with you. You belong to me."

This happened before humanity lifted a finger.

Blessing was not a reward for obedience; it was the foundation for existence.

You don't earn this covering; you receive it because you exist.

As the sermon proclaims:

"Before you did anything right or wrong, before you succeeded or stumbled, you were already covered in grace."

Covered Through Your Mistakes

It's crucial to understand: this covering is continuous, not conditional.

You were blessed at the beginning *knowing* you would make mistakes along the way.

In fact, Genesis itself proves this:

- In chapter 2, humanity is given the command not to eat from the tree.
- In chapter 3, they eat it anyway.
- And in chapter 4, they're still alive, raising children.

Why?

Because the blessing of chapter 1 never expired.

The covering of *barak* was stronger than their disobedience.

Their failure did not erase their favor.

And neither does yours.

Your story does not end at your mistakes because you are still covered.

Covered With Purpose

This covering is not just protection, it's also empowerment.

It reminds you that you are never alone in carrying your cause.

It reassures you that you can rise again when you fall.

It gives you courage to walk in the fullness of who you were created to be.

Even when you wander off, even when you feel unworthy, even when others abandon you, the One who formed you never withdraws covering.

The Blessing Still Holds

So many of us live as if we have to re-earn God's love, as if our missteps have nullified the blessing.

But you cannot lose what you never earned.

You didn't deserve it then, and you don't disqualify yourself now.

The blessing was placed on you at the beginning, and it remains.

The sermon put it this way:

"You may have done foolish things, but you're still here because you were covered from creation. Every chapter of your life is possible because of the blessing of chapter one."

You were not sent into the world naked and alone.

You were wrapped in *barak*, the blessing of divine presence, approval, and favor.

Even when you fall, you fall into hands that hold you.

Even when you fail, you fail under the canopy of grace.

Even when you forget who you are, the covering remains.

You are held.

You are blessed.

You are still covered.

Mirror Work - You Were Created to Be Covered Continuously

Look at yourself gently, smile if you can, and say:

"I am covered. I was blessed before I performed, loved before I proved anything, and held even when I fell. The blessing never left me. I am still covered in grace, still wrapped in favor."

Write down one area of your life where you've felt abandoned or uncovered, and then write the truth: *"Even here, I am covered."*

Reminder:

You don't have to earn the blessing, you just have to believe it.

You don't have to work for what was already placed on you.

You are covered continuously, no matter what.

Closing Reflection:

Take a moment to breathe deeply and let these truths settle in your spirit.

You were consciously created, not an accident but a masterpiece.

You were made as a copy of the Creator, carrying divine appearance, attributes, and authority.

You were created completely, with everything you need already inside of you.

You were created for community, to thrive in connection with others.

You were created for a cause, to live out your unique assignment in the world.

And you were created to be covered continuously, blessed before you even began.

You don't have to chase what you already carry.

You don't have to perform for approval you already possess.

You don't have to prove a worth you already embody.

Stop rehearsing who you are not, and start reclaiming who you already are.

Reflection Questions:

- Who or what has made you doubt that you are "very good"?

_____

_____

_____

_____

_____

- In which areas of your life are you striving to earn what is already yours?

_____

_____

_____

_____

_____

- How would your relationships, your work, and your self-talk change if you truly believed you are already whole, covered, and enough?

_____

_____

_____

_____

_____

- What parts of your identity have you ignored or hidden because of shame or comparison?

  _____

  _____

  _____

  _____

  _____

- How can you begin to activate what's already inside of you this week?

  _____

  _____

  _____

  _____

  _____

Scripture Meditation
Genesis 1:31
"God saw all that had been made, and it was very good. And there was evening, and there was morning, the sixth day."

Prayer:

Creator, who thought of me before I breathed a single breath, who crafted me with care and called me "very good," I pause now to remember who I am. I release the lies I've believed, the shame I've carried, and the masks I've worn. I choose to see Your image reflected in me. Help me walk boldly in the blessing You placed on me from the beginning. Thank You for covering me when I stumbled, for waiting patiently as I wandered, and for loving me without condition. Today, I remember: I am Yours. I am enough. I am covered. Amen.

CHAPTER 9

FIXING FLAWED FORMATION, TAKING OFF WHAT NO LONGER SERVES YOU

Text: Exodus 3:4–5

Before you can step into who you were created to be, you must first confront who you became just to survive. Many of us are living in shoes we were never meant to wear, shoes worn thin by trauma, titles, expectations, and lies. These shoes have walked us through seasons of pain, but they cannot take us into our purpose.

That is what this chapter is about: confronting the ways you were formed and bravely taking off what no longer serves you.

The Problem of Formation

Identity does not just happen; it is formed. From the moment you entered the world, you were being shaped by family, culture, trauma, achievement, failure, and even silence. Every look, every word, every experience imprinted something into you.

But here is the hard truth: just because you were formed does not mean you were formed correctly. Like Moses, many of us carry a flawed formation, a mix of abandonment, arrogance, insecurity, and performance. Moses grew up split between two worlds,

Hebrew by birth, Egyptian by upbringing, and neither seemed to fully claim him.

By the time we meet him in Exodus 3, he is wandering in Midian, a fugitive from his past and a stranger to himself. But then God interrupts his wandering with a burning bush, and everything changes.

God Confronts Our Flawed Formation

The bush was burning, but it wasn't consumed. And a voice called out, "Moses, Moses." When Moses responded, God told him: *"Do not come any closer. Take off your sandals, for the place where you are standing is holy ground" (Exodus 3:5).*

GOD's initial request of Moses is to remove his sandals. This may seem like a weird request, but GOD had some intentionality with it. GOD knew that the man who stood before him, yes was the man he needed, but not in the present flawed formed state he was in. He was wearing sandals that expressed a status that was fashioned, but not formed. It was a facade that masked and hid the wounds, the hurt and the confusion of his past. He looked whole and strong, but GOD knew that this was just an act. So the first thing GOD wanted him to do was remove his sandals, his accoutrement, his shell. GOD knew what those sandals represented. GOD knew that everything Moses had been through, every experience he had prior to that moment, and GOD was saying "before you have an encounter with me, before I can properly use you, you have to remove from yourself everything that led to this moment."

You maybe are reading this and understand completely. If you are honest with yourself and have your mirror nearby, you probably understand what it is like to appear whole to the world, to dress up, to cover up your internal pain, but who you show is not really the substance of who you are. You are simply presenting a show. You are, "putting your best foot forward," but really you are broken, hurting, and empty. GOD may be speaking to you in this very moment. GOD may be saying to you, to take your sandals off, for the ground you are standing on is HOLY ground. It is a sacred, real, and reforming ground, for you need to be reformed.

This was not just a physical act, it was symbolic. Moses' sandals represented the flawed formation he'd been carrying:

- **Early Abandonment**

  Moses' story begins with being placed in a basket and sent down the river. Though it was done to save him, that experience of being "sent away" left an imprint of abandonment. He grew up without the daily presence of his parents, without the affirmation of belonging to his own people. Many of us have a similar wound, being left physically, emotionally, or spiritually by those who were supposed to protect and nurture us. Even when we intellectually understand *why* it happened, our hearts often internalize the message: *"You're not worth staying for."* That lie can shape how we see ourselves and how we relate to others, clinging too tightly to people, or refusing to let anyone get too close.

- **Emotional Absence**

  Even though Moses grew up in Pharaoh's palace, surrounded by wealth and status, he lived in emotional exile. His needs for connection and understanding went unmet in an environment that valued performance and appearances over authentic feeling. Many of us grew up the same way, with parents who provided materially but were unavailable emotionally. We learned to suppress our feelings to avoid conflict, to numb our pain rather than express it. That emotional absence often leaves us with an ache we can't name, feeling lonely even in a room full of people, and afraid of showing vulnerability because we don't trust it will be met with care.

- ## Educational Arrogance

  Raised and educated in all the wisdom of Egypt, Moses came to believe that knowledge and competence would shield him from failure. His education gave him tools, but it also fed his ego, convincing him he could fix problems in his own strength. Many of us have done the same, pursuing degrees, titles, and achievements to prove we are enough. Yet when our competence fails to heal our wounds, we are left confused and disillusioned. Education and skill are valuable, but when they become our identity, they can harden into pride and keep us from depending on the One who truly equips us.

- ## Entitled Aggression

  Moses' inner conflict erupted in violence when he killed the Egyptian overseer. His sense of justice was good, but his method was destructive. This entitled aggression, the belief that his pain justified his rage, left him alienated and on the run. Likewise, our own woundedness can manifest as anger, defensiveness, or controlling behavior. We think striking out will restore our power, but it only deepens our exile. Healing begins when we acknowledge the anger underneath our aggression and allow it to be transformed rather than unleashed.

God called Moses to remove his sandals because what carried him here could not carry him forward. And the same is true for you.

Fixing Flawed Formation, The Journey Begins

Before Moses could step into his calling, he had to unlearn the false lessons of his formation. Though he was chosen and created with purpose, the environments he grew up in had shaped him in ways that conflicted with who God said he was. The palace taught him privilege but not empathy. His pain taught him anger but not healing. His isolation taught him survival but not trust.

We are no different. Even though we were consciously created and divinely commissioned, many of us were also deeply shaped, even distorted, by flawed formation. Those distortions may have protected us in a toxic environment, but they no longer serve us. They block us from intimacy with God, with others, and even with ourselves.

That's why God invited Moses to the burning bush and instructed him to *take off his sandals*. It was a symbolic and spiritual act: shedding what no longer belonged, removing what carried the dust of the wrong journey. It was the first of several steps toward wholeness.

Fixing flawed formation is not about erasing the past, it is about confronting it honestly, grieving what was lost or broken, and courageously letting go of what no longer aligns with God's intention for you.

In the next section, we explore four common elements of flawed formation that many of us carry, and how to begin removing them so that our true selves can emerge.

Steps Toward Fixing Flawed Formation
Remove What Reminds You

God said, *"Take off your sandals."* Sandals protect your feet from what you're walking on, but they also carry the dust of everywhere you've been. For Moses, his sandals held the memories of Egypt, the mistakes he made, and the man he no longer wanted to be. These sandals were developed over time. Moses was 40 years old when he fled Egypt, and had spent another 40 years in Midian, and now on Mount Horeb, Moses was 80 plus years. That is 80 plus years of memories, of pain, of survival, with the residue from all of those situations compounded in and on his sandals.

What are you carrying? What memories are you harboring and hiding? What is anchoring you and providing the foundation you have build your house of card on? Oftentime for survival we suppress what almost destroyed us. We suppress the memories, trauma, and pain. We don't have time to deal with and address them, so we attempt to silence them until they show up in inopportune moments often under stress, but in an attempt to future save us or to show our strength, but due to their improperness or their immaturity, they often make our situation worse.

What Reminders Are You Still Wearing?

When God told Moses to *take off his sandals*, it was not just about respect for holy ground, it was about shedding the remnants of everywhere he had been that was not aligned with where he was going. Sandals in that culture carried the dust, dirt, and debris of every path walked before. They held the memories of Egypt, the wilderness, and even the shame of running away.

What about you?

What "sandals" are you still wearing, what habits, attitudes, or symbols are you carrying, that still track the dust of past pain and flawed formation into your present?

Maybe you're still wearing the shoes of bitterness, walking into every new relationship expecting betrayal because of what happened before.

Maybe you're still wearing the shoes of people-pleasing, carrying the belief that your worth comes from making everyone else happy.

Maybe you're still wearing the shoes of self-sabotage, walking out of opportunities before anyone else can reject you.

Maybe you're still wearing the shoes of comparison, lacing them tighter every time you scroll through someone else's highlight reel online.

God is saying: *Take those shoes off.* You can't walk into the next season of your calling if you keep tracking the dust of old wounds all over it.

The dust of Egypt has no place on holy ground.

This isn't just about letting go of visible behaviors, it's about naming the invisible agreements you've made along the way: "I'll never trust again." "I'll always have to fight for myself." "I'm not worthy of love." Those are sandals too, worn-out, ill-fitting, and heavy with lies.

In this moment, imagine yourself at the burning bush. You are on holy ground. You've been seen and called by the One who created you. And now you hear the instruction clearly: *Remove what reminds you. Take off what no longer fits. Step into this sacred space barefoot, unburdened, and ready for something new.*

To fix your flawed formation, you must first strip away the symbols of where you've been.

Mirror Work - Remove What Reminds You

Stand in front of the mirror and gently look at yourself. Say:

"I see the dust I've been carrying, memories, mistakes, labels, but today, I choose to wipe them off. I name what no longer fits, and I release it. The dust of Egypt cannot cover my calling. I am stepping barefoot into what's next."

Take a moment to list, either aloud or in writing, the specific "shoes" you've worn too long: bitterness, people-pleasing, comparison, or shame, and imagine setting them down at your feet. Breathe deeply, and feel the weight lift.

Shed What Stops You

God asked Moses to come closer but not as he was. GOD asked Moses to remove his sandals. Sandals in those day were a sign of status. Sandals separated the slaves from the slave owners. Persons

151

who wore sandals had wealth. Their wealth, titles, and status make them feel set-apart, and often become a barrier to their submission and pursuit of GOD. Often we are hungry for GOD until we get from GOD what we prayed about to GOD. But, GOD says, "Take them sandals off because they are preventing you from experiencing the fullness of ME." They have cause you to change who you were to start becoming who you were never created to be.

If you would be honest, your possessions and your achievements have shifted your perspective of yourself and have allowed you to hide your hurt and your pain behind their attainment. Your titles, status, and pride cannot stand on holy ground. For Moses, his royal upbringing and self-importance had become barriers to intimacy with God.

In the same way, we too must shed what stops us from fully surrendering, including internal burdens we've mistaken for survival tools.

The Belief We Have to Earn Love

So many of us walk into holy spaces with the silent conviction that we must earn God's affection, approval, and acceptance. It is the mistaken act of performance. We tend to perform and do thinking that will get us noticed and that will get us appreciated. That belief makes us perform for love rather than simply receive it. It keeps us running on a treadmill of "good works," exhausting ourselves to prove we're enough, when the truth is, love was ours before we did anything at all. To shed this belief is to finally rest in the reality that love is a gift, not a wage.

The Mask of Perfectionism

Perfectionism is a polished shield we wear to keep people, and God, from seeing our flaws. We think if we're flawless, we'll be accepted. So we are afraid to show our real selves. We take all of our energy to pop out and be great, and hate ourselves for any behavior, action, or act that is less than stellar. We are hiding, but that mask hardens us and distances us from real intimacy. Shedding it means allowing ourselves to be seen, imperfect, in process, and beloved anyway. It means stepping barefoot into the presence of the One who already knows and welcomes us as we are.

The Pressure to Maintain an Image

Some of us feel trapped by the persona we've built, the titles, roles, and reputations we think we must uphold. We carry the weight of other people's expectations on our shoulders, afraid that letting it drop will reveal how human we really are. But holy ground is no place for facades. Shedding this pressure frees us to step into our calling authentically, not as a brand, but as a beloved being.

God's invitation to surrender is an invitation to take all of that off, the belief you have to earn love, the mask of perfectionism, and the pressure to maintain an image, and walk barefoot into sacred presence.

It may have served you once, but it is stopping you now.

Mirror Work - Shed What Stops You

Face the mirror and reflect honestly:

"I no longer need to perform to earn love. I no longer need perfection to feel worthy. I no longer need to hold up an image that hides my truth. I am seen, accepted, and loved exactly as I am, even barefoot and vulnerable before God."

Close your eyes for a few seconds, and when you open them again, look at yourself with kindness and imagine taking off the mask of perfection, the heavy robes of others' expectations, and standing simply and authentically in God's presence.

Take Off What Hasn't Transformed You

It's amazing that GOD counted on Moses' nack for sticking his nose in other people's business to cause him to pay attention to the burning bush. What do I mean. Well, it was Moses' nosy behavior that got him in the situation of killing the Egyptian task master. It was his nosey behavior that had him interfere with the two Hebrews arguing leading to him fleeing Egypt. It was his nosiness that had him interfere with the affairs of persons at the well in Midian, and GOD knew that that same behavior would be displayed if he just consumed the bush with fire. Some of us wear old behaviors like badges, even though they haven't made us better. Moses had a pattern of proving himself, through violence, flight, and hiding, yet none of it healed him.

When Moses stood at the burning bush, the voice of the Divine told him: *"Take off your sandals, for the place where you are standing is holy ground"* (Exodus 3:5). Why the sandals? Because they symbolized the journey he had walked up until that moment, a journey full of survival tactics, broken cycles, and self-protection. Those sandals had carried him through shame, fear, hiding, and wandering. But now he was standing before God, and the ground itself demanded something more honest, something more surrendered.

We, too, carry things into holy spaces that have protected us but never perfected us, habits, identities, and beliefs that helped us survive but never transformed us. If they haven't healed you, haven't made you more whole, haven't brought you closer to who God created you to be, it's time to take them off.

Here are some examples of what this looks like in real life:

Repeated Patterns

We often hold on to behaviors and habits because they feel familiar, even when they harm us. Like Moses striking down the Egyptian, or fleeing into the wilderness, we repeat actions that seem to help in the moment but leave us stuck. Taking off what hasn't transformed you means identifying those cycles, of anger, avoidance, sabotage, or silence, and saying: *"This doesn't serve who I'm becoming anymore."*

Recurring Problems

Some of us wear our problems like badges of honor. We let wounds define us. We keep bringing the same drama into every relationship, every opportunity, every room we walk into. But if it keeps you tied to old pain and prevents you from growing, it's not holy, it's heavy. Taking it off is a declaration: *"I refuse to keep carrying what keeps wounding me."*

Remedial Proving

This one is subtle but deadly. We feel like we have to prove ourselves, to God, to others, even to ourselves, over and over again. We keep running the same race, fighting the same battles, trying to earn what's already been given. But transformation doesn't come from performing. It comes from trusting that you are already loved, already chosen, already called.

When God called Moses to take off his sandals, it wasn't just about showing respect, it was about letting go. Letting go of Egypt. Letting go of Midian. Letting go of every false identity and empty pattern he had been wearing.

And so for us, the question becomes:

What habits or patterns am I still wearing even though they haven't changed me for the better?

What pain am I carrying that God is inviting me to set down?

What image of myself do I need to release to step fully into who I really am?

Holy ground demands honesty. Holy ground demands humility. Holy ground demands that we leave behind what has not made us whole, and step barefoot into the presence of the One who can.

Mirror Work - Take Off What Hasn't Transformed You

Look yourself in the eyes and say:

"These habits and patterns got me here, but they cannot take me further. I refuse to wear what keeps me stuck. I lay down what hasn't healed me. I release what looks strong but leaves me empty. Today, I choose to be honest, humble, and whole."

Write down three patterns, roles, or grudges you've clung to, and next to each, write what it would feel like to let it go. Then say aloud:

"I release these old shoes. I stand barefoot, ready for what is holy, ready to be re-formed."

Sidebar Takeaway:
Holy Ground Demands Bare Feet

Moses couldn't fully encounter the Divine until he removed the dust-covered symbols of his wandering. Likewise, you can't step fully into who you are while clinging to what you were.

- ☑ Let go of repeated patterns that keep you stuck.
- ☑ Lay down recurring problems that define your identity.
- ☑ Stop trying to prove what God has already declared.

When what you're wearing no longer honors where you're standing, it's time to take it off.

It's time to take off what hasn't transformed you:

- The addiction you justified as "just stress."
- The unhealthy relationship you stayed in for fear of being alone.
- The anger you carried as armor.

If it hasn't brought you closer to God, closer to healing, closer to wholeness, take it off.

Mirror Moment:

What have you been wearing that looks strong but leaves you empty?

God Can Use Your Flaws

Here is the grace: God is not surprised by your flawed formation. In fact, God intends to redeem it. The same curiosity that led Moses to the bush, the same boldness that got him into trouble, the same longing to belong, God repurposed it all.

You don't have to hide your flaws; you just have to bring them to the fire. The bush was burning but not consumed, and you can be too.

Taking Off Your Shoes

When Moses took off his shoes, he wasn't just obeying a command, he was saying:

"I am done pretending. I am done hiding. I am done carrying Egypt on my feet. I stand barefoot before You, ready to be re-formed."

That is your invitation too. Stand on holy ground. Feel it under your feet. Take off what no longer belongs and let God re-form you.

Reminder:

Before you move forward, pause and let this sink in: you cannot take Egypt into the Promised Land. You cannot carry the wilderness into your next chapter. What carried you here can't carry you there..

Reflection Questions:

- What flawed formations have shaped your sense of self?

  _____

  _____

  _____

  _____

  _____

- What reminders (habits, objects, nicknames) keep you tied to your old story?

  _____

  _____

  _____

  _____

  _____

- What would it look like for you to "take off your shoes" today?

  _____

  _____

  _____

  _____

  _____

- How have you confused survival skills for your true identity, and what would it mean to lay them down?

  _____

  _____

  _____

  _____

  _____

- In what ways have your "sandals" (titles, habits, defenses) been protecting you from pain but also keeping you from purpose?

  _____

  _____

  _____

  _____

  _____

- What would stepping barefoot on holy ground, fully vulnerable and honest before God, look like for you right now?

  _____

  _____

  _____

  _____

  _____

- Who might you become if you trusted God enough to let go of what you've outgrown?

_____

_____

_____

_____

_____

Scripture Meditation
Exodus 3:5
"Take off your sandals, for the place where you are standing is holy ground."

Prayer:

God, I confess that I have worn my flawed formation like a badge. Help me take it off. Remove everything in me that does not reflect who You created me to be. Teach me to walk barefoot in Your presence, vulnerable, whole, and surrendered. Amen.

Sidebar: 3 Keys to Fixing Flawed Formation

- God is not surprised by your flaws; they are part of your journey toward healing.

- The ground you're standing on is already holy, but you can only stand barefoot.

- You are not disqualified; you are still called by name.

CHAPTER 10

I KNOW WHO I AM, STANDING IN THE POWER OF YOUR IDENTITY

Text: Luke 4:16–21

"The Spirit of the Lord is upon me, because the Lord has anointed me..."

It is becoming more evident that many people are suffering from an identity crisis. You see it everywhere: people constantly seeking validation from social media, counting likes, shares, comments, and retweets, as if their worth can be tallied in the approval of others. They make drastic changes, post curated moments, or even stir controversy, all in the hope of being seen, affirmed, and celebrated. They are always seeking the approval of others because they are insecure in themselves. Insecurity leads us to reach outward for what can only be affirmed inward.

But there is something powerful, freeing even, about knowing who you are. There is something unshakable about standing firmly in your being, aware of your flaws, your strengths, your boundaries, and your worth. This security does not come from outward opinions but from an intrinsic understanding of your God-given identity.

This chapter is to fuel your desire to find your purpose. This chapter is to remind you that there is an assignment that you have that

161

noone else is able to do, and you must know it, stand firm on it, and complete it.

Before we even enter the chapter, consider this: even Jesus went through serious formational experiences that helped establish Him and His confidence in His identity. Yes, He was fully divine, the Word made flesh, but from a human perspective, Jesus' confidence was cultivated through His experiences, affirmations, and choices. He had to know who He was to walk on water, heal the sick, cast out demons, stand up to religious leaders, and even rebuke His closest disciples when necessary. That kind of boldness was rooted in self-identity, grounded in positive affirmation not based on performance.

The Journey to Knowing Who You Are

As you begin this chapter, pause and reflect on your own journey toward knowing yourself. What wildernesses have you endured? What voices have shaped you, for better or worse? The path to understanding who you truly are is rarely straight; it weaves through doubts, battles, silence, and surrender. But here is the good news: God is not waiting for you to achieve perfection before affirming you. Instead, God meets you in your humanity and reveals your identity in the process.

In Luke 4:16–21, Jesus stands in the synagogue of His hometown, opens the scroll of Isaiah, and boldly declares His identity and His mission: *"The Spirit of the Lord is upon me…"* This is no performance for applause, in fact, many reject Him. This is about affirming what heaven already declared: you are chosen, anointed, and enough.

Like Jesus, you must learn to stand in the power of your identity, even when others doubt you, even when it is uncomfortable. This chapter is about reclaiming your voice, silencing false narratives, and standing boldly in who you are. So how do you develop a strong self-identity.

Positive Affirmations Without Performance

Self-identity comes from positive affirmation that is not based on performance. We see this beautifully illustrated in Luke 3:22, when Jesus is baptized: *"The Holy Spirit descended in bodily form like a dove upon him, and a voice came from heaven which said, 'You are my beloved Son; in you I am well pleased.'"* Notice: before Jesus performed a single miracle, before He taught a single parable or healed a single person, the voice from heaven affirmed Him.

This is a profound truth, and a challenge for us. We often tie our worth to what we produce or accomplish. Many of us operate in what can be called *transactional affirmation*: we feel worthy only when we succeed, when we impress, when we perform. But God's affirmation of Jesus came before any of that. It came before He "earned" anything.

This is the kind of affirmation that sustains you when the crowds are silent, when applause fades, when your performance falters. You are loved simply because you are. The voice of God declared Jesus beloved in private, not in front of the masses. Likewise, your identity cannot depend on public applause, because people are fickle. They may praise you one moment and criticize you the next. But the affirmation that comes from God is stable, unchanging, and unconditional.

Imagine how different your life would be if you truly believed that your worth is not tied to your work. That even if you never earned another degree, never won another award, never gained another follower, you would still be fully seen, fully loved, and fully enough.

Jesus' confidence was not rooted in what He did, but in who He was. And that is the foundation you need as well.

Mirror Work - Positive Affirmations Without Performance

Stand in the mirror and say aloud:

"I am beloved by God, not because of what I do, but because of who I am. Even without achievements, I am already enough. Heaven affirmed me before the crowd ever noticed me."

Self-Discovery Through Severe Difficulty and Drama

Not only does self-identity come from positive affirmation, but self-discovery often comes through drama and difficulty. Right after His baptism, after being publicly affirmed, Jesus was "full of the Holy Spirit" and led into the wilderness, where He was tested for 40 days by the devil (Luke 4:1–2). This testing was not a contradiction to His calling, it was confirmation.

Many of us imagine that once we know who we are, the journey becomes easy. But in reality, discovering who you truly are often happens in the wilderness of adversity. It is through difficulty that our identity is refined and revealed.

After His baptism, Jesus learned firsthand what it meant to live out what God had already declared about Him. The wilderness tested whether He truly believed He was the beloved Son. Likewise, your own discovery of who you are often emerges through seasons of resistance and refining. You don't know how strong your faith is until it's challenged. You don't know how much grace you carry until you're stretched beyond your comfort zone. It is the furnace of testing that reveals the gold of your character.

Think about the jobs you thought you couldn't handle, the losses you thought you wouldn't survive, the obstacles you thought were insurmountable, yet here you are. Your trials did not define you, but they did reveal you.

Your identity is not only declared at the river but discovered in the desert. Both the affirmation and the adversity work together to uncover the fullness of who you are.

Mirror Work - Self-Discovery Through Severe Difficulty and Drama

Look yourself in the eyes and reflect:

"What wildernesses shaped me? What trials revealed my true strength? Even in difficulty, I am discovering who I really am. I thank God for refining me through adversity."

Self- Esteem increased after Surviving the Enemy

Lastly, self-esteem grows when you survive encounters with the enemy. In Luke 4:13–14, after Jesus overcame the devil's temptations, the text says: *"When the devil had ended every temptation, he departed from him until an opportune time. Then Jesus returned in the power of the Spirit to Galilee."*

Jesus emerged from His testing stronger, more confident, and fully aware of His authority. Likewise, when you survive what was meant to break you, your confidence deepens. Every test you've overcome, every wrong you've endured, every battle you've won, has strengthened your resolve. You walk differently after you've faced the enemy and lived to tell the story.

Your "swagger" changes because you've seen what you're capable of enduring. You know you're still standing, not because it was easy, but because God's Spirit strengthened you. The things that once intimidated you no longer hold power over you. You've discovered resilience you didn't know you had, and that resilience fuels your confidence for the next battle.

If you hadn't survived what you did, you'd still be cowering in fear, but now you stand tall, knowing that what couldn't kill you has only made you stronger.

Mirror Work - Self-Esteem Increased After Surviving the Enemy

Take a deep breath in front of the mirror and declare:

"What was meant to destroy me only made me stronger. I survived what others thought I wouldn't. I stand here today because God's Spirit carried me through every battle."

The Evidence of Knowing Who You Are

So now we find ourselves a little further into the story. Jesus is in the synagogue. He unrolls the scroll, reads Isaiah's prophecy, rolls it back up, and confidently declares, "Today this Scripture has been fulfilled in your hearing." In other words, He tells them plainly: *"I know who I am."*

And when you know who you are, there is evidence, visible, undeniable, and powerful. Your confidence shows up in how you walk, speak, decide, and even how you endure. There are marks of someone who has discovered their identity, and those marks cannot be faked. When you know who you are, you stand in your truth even when others doubt it.

When Jesus spoke those words, He wasn't seeking approval. He wasn't asking permission. He was standing in what He already knew to be true. The question is, do you know who you are? Do you know how to know, how to tell that you are secure in your identity? There should be some signs that you are secure in who you are.

You can Stand in the Presence of the Familiar and not be Fazed.

When you know who you are, you can stand in the presence of the familiar and not be fazed. In Luke 4:16, Jesus returns to Nazareth, His hometown, surrounded by people who knew His history, His family, and even the whispers about His legitimacy. These were the same people who remembered Him as "just Mary's son," "Joseph's boy," or "the carpenter."

For many of us, standing before those who knew us before we grew into ourselves can feel unsettling. Familiar faces often remind us of our past mistakes, our childhood vulnerabilities, or the rumors that once defined us. They may even doubt your transformation, unable or unwilling to see the growth within you.

Yet Jesus stood unshaken. Though they whispered and questioned, He boldly unrolled the scroll and proclaimed His calling. This shows us that knowing who you are enables you to face the familiar, the doubters, the skeptics, even your own past, without faltering. Their whispers do not define you. Their memories of who you were cannot diminish who you are becoming.

When you know who you are, their gossip fuels your determination rather than shakes your resolve. You no longer shrink in rooms full of doubt; you stand tall because your confidence is rooted in something deeper than their opinions.

Mirror Work - Standing in the Presence of the Familiar and Not Being Fazed

Gaze into the mirror and affirm:

"I am no longer defined by who they used to say I was. Their memories of my past don't diminish my present. I can stand tall even among those who once doubted me."

Speak Up for Yourself Based on Who GOD says You Are

Not only does identity begin with positive affirmation not tied to performance, it also requires you to speak up for yourself based on what God says, not what people say. In Luke 3:22, at His baptism,

Jesus hears: *"You are my beloved Son; in you I am well pleased."* Notice this affirmation came before Jesus performed a single miracle.

We often live on *transactional affirmation*: believing we must earn love and acceptance through what we do. But God's affirmation is not transactional, it is foundational. Many of us still let people define us, chasing their approval instead of embracing what God already declared.

When Jesus unrolled the scroll in the synagogue, He didn't just pick any passage. He went straight to what we now know as Isaiah 61. Remember, there were no chapters or verses then, just long scrolls of text. Yet Jesus bypassed the powerful verses of Isaiah 6 ("In the year King Uzziah died…") and Isaiah 7 ("A virgin shall conceive…") and Isaiah 40 ("They that wait on the Lord shall renew their strength…"). Instead, He chose the passage that explicitly spoke to His mission and identity.

Why? Because He knew who He was. And because He knew, He spoke. He didn't let the whispers of others define Him. He spoke up for Himself using the Word as His reference point.

To speak up for yourself like Jesus:

- You must study the Word so you know what it says about you.

- You must believe what it says, that you are more than a conqueror, fearfully and wonderfully made, created in God's image.

- You must speak it over yourself, even when the crowd says otherwise.

When Jesus asked His disciples in Matthew 16, *"Who do people say I am?"*, they rattled off others' confused opinions. But then He pressed, *"Who do you say I am?"*, inviting them to name the truth. Stop letting others write your narrative. Stop chasing approval from the crowd. Define yourself by what God has already spoken. Stand in who God says you are.

Mirror Work - Speaking Up for Yourself Based on Who GOD Says You Are

In the mirror, say boldly:

"I speak what God has already spoken about me. His Word defines me, not the whispers of others. I will not stay silent when God has already affirmed me."

Know Your Identity is not Dependent on other Individuals.

You must be secure in knowing your identity is not dependent on individuals. Look closely at Luke 4:18, Jesus declares: *"The Spirit of the Lord is upon me because the Lord has anointed me…"* Here, He boldly tells the crowd: "I was selected by God. God chose me and equipped me. You did not place me here, and you cannot remove me."

Often, people believe they have power over you because they think they put you in position. But your calling, your gifts, and your identity are not determined by human hands. They are divine. Jesus' confidence came from knowing that no one else's opinion or vote could validate or invalidate what God already ordained.

In church, in family, in work, people may believe their approval is what holds you up. But you must be secure enough to say: "I am here because God chose me, God equipped me, and God placed me. What God has for me is mine."

Your identity is not created or destroyed by the applause of others. It is anchored in the One who created you. You are predestined, preordained, and prepared by God. This is why you've survived the tests. This is why you've endured the trials. Because you were being equipped for what was already yours.

When you know who you are in God:

- You stop chasing applause from the crowd.

- You stop fearing their withdrawal of support.
- You stand firm, knowing your worth and assignment come from God.

As Colossians 3:23 reminds us: *"Whatever you do, do it heartily as unto the Lord and not to men, knowing that from the Lord you will receive the inheritance as your reward."*

Be secure. Be steadfast. Be unshaken, because God already approved you.

Mirror Work - Knowing Your Identity Is Not Dependent on Other Individuals

Look at yourself and say:

"I am here because God chose and equipped me, not because of anyone else. No one can take away what God has placed in me. My calling is secure in Him."

State Your Assignment, Even if It Doesn't Appease or Please the Popular

When you know who you are, you can state your assignment even when it doesn't align with what is popular. Jesus declared that His mission was to bring good news to the poor, healing to the brokenhearted, freedom to the captive, sight to the blind, and liberty to the oppressed. Notice that His focus was not on appeasing the powerful or pleasing the popular but serving those in need.

His assignment, to preach to the marginalized, to heal the hurting, to liberate the oppressed, was radical and countercultural. It wasn't designed to win Him friends in high places or garner Him applause from the elite. Rather, it unsettled the comfortable and challenged the status quo.

When you boldly state your purpose and refuse to shrink or shift to fit others' preferences, the room may fall silent, as it did when

Jesus finished reading and all eyes were on Him. But silence doesn't mean rejection. It means the truth has landed.

Be prepared: your calling may take you to places where others won't go, to people others won't serve, and to causes others avoid. Being faithful to your assignment will sometimes cost you popularity, but it will ground you more deeply in purpose.

Your validation is not based on their applause. It comes from your anointing.

Mirror Work - Stating Your Assignment, Even if It Doesn't Please the Popular

Face the mirror with courage and declare:

"I will stand in my assignment even when it makes others uncomfortable. My purpose is not to please crowds but to serve God and those He's called me to."

Start Showing what You Been Saying

Finally, when you know who you are, you don't just speak it, you show it. After reading the scroll and declaring His identity, Jesus sat down and said: *"Today, this Scripture is fulfilled in your hearing."* Then He began living it out, casting out demons, healing the sick, and embodying the good news He proclaimed.

It's not enough to declare your identity with words alone. You must demonstrate it through actions. Jesus proved who He was not by arguing or self-promoting but by showing up in power, serving faithfully, and glorifying God through His deeds.

When you know who you are:

- You stop performing for approval and start living purposefully.
- You let your actions silence the doubters.

- You understand that the power working through you is not your own but comes from the Holy Spirit.

You don't have to prove anything to people, only to honor the One who entrusted you with purpose. Every day is an opportunity to confirm that God didn't waste breath, power, or Spirit in creating and equipping you. Your assignment is not about self-promotion but about glorifying God and building up the community.

So stop chasing likes. Stop trying to please everyone. Operate boldly in who you were created to be, because God has already declared you enough.

Mirror Work - Start Showing What You've Been Saying

End in front of the mirror by saying:

"I will live out what I declare. My actions will align with my identity. I don't need to prove anything to others, my life already reflects God's glory and goodness."

Reflection Questions

- In what ways have you sought validation from others instead of resting in your God-given identity?

_____

_____

_____

_____

_____

- What false definitions, from family, culture, or failure, have you internalized?

_____

_____

_____

_____

_____

- Where in your life has fear kept you silent or small?

_____

_____

_____

_____

_____

- What wilderness season in your life most shaped your understanding of who you are?

_____

_____

_____

_____

_____

- Where have you allowed the opinions of others to silence the truth God already spoke over you?

_____

_____

_____

_____

_____

- How would your choices change if you truly believed you are already loved and approved by God?

_____

_____

_____

_____

_____

- What "scroll" would you unroll, what mission statement could you declare, about your calling right now?

_____

_____

_____

_____

_____

- How have you seen your past battles strengthen your confidence to stand in rooms that once intimidated you?

_____

_____

_____

_____

_____

- What action can you take this week to demonstrate your identity rather than just speak about it?

_____

_____

_____

_____

_____

Scripture Meditation
Luke 4:18
"The Spirit of the Lord is upon me, because the Lord has anointed me..."

Prayer

Creator, thank You for affirming me before I performed, finding me in my wilderness, and strengthening me through battle. Help me stand confidently, speak boldly, and live faithfully in who You say I am. Amen.

Sidebar: 7 Evidences You Know Who You Are

- You stand unshaken in the presence of doubt.
- You declare God's Word as your definition.
- You remain secure even when others leave.
- You clearly state your assignment without apology.
- You show your identity through action, not just words.
- You set boundaries that reflect your worth.
- You pursue purpose over popularity.

CHAPTER 11

MORE THAN MEETS THE EYE, LIVING BEYOND WHAT THEY SEE

Text: Romans 8:35–39

Before we even open Romans 8, let's name what we're up against.

When I say *More Than Meets the Eye*, I'm borrowing from the Transformers' tagline, ordinary vehicles that, under pressure, revealed their true power and identity. At first glance, they looked unremarkable, but inside was strength no one could see.

Identity doesn't just tell us who we are, it reminds us that we are more than meets the eye. We are never unloved, never overcome, never counted out. Not by distress. Not by destruction. Not by distraction. Not even by death. Identity is the armor that keeps us covered even when everything else falls apart.

Saboteur vs. Scripture:

Saboteur: *"You're alone."*

Scripture: *"Nothing shall separate us from the love of God." (Romans 8:39)*

Many of us live like we're defeated because we've internalized lies about who we are. We carry ourselves as though forgotten or forsaken. But Romans 8 invites us to the mirror to see ourselves as God sees us, more than what meets the eye.

This is mirror work: standing before your reflection, releasing false labels, and embracing your true identity. What you see in the mirror isn't all there is, your worth is more than your wounds, more than others' words, more than your worries. Your blessing isn't about possessions but about knowing the God who never leaves you, equips you to stand, and works all things for your good.

So as you come out of the previous chapter where you declared who you are, this chapter invites you to believe it, deeply, even when circumstances try to contradict it.

This chapter is where you solidify who you are as confirmed by the challenges you face and the conditions you find your elf in. You know who you are and now it's time to walk fully in it. Your identity remains secure. You are more than meets the eye.

Even in hardship, you are never unloved. Even under pressure, you are never powerless. Even in the valley, you are never alone.

So as you begin this chapter, stand before the mirror of Romans 8 and hear this:

You are not what others whisper about you.

You are not what your circumstances suggest.

You are not the sum of your mistakes or your fears.

You are *more than meets the eye*, because of the One who sees it all.

This is what it mean to be more than meets the eye!!!

You Are Never Unloved (Romans 8:35)

Paul asks, *"Who shall separate us from the love of Christ?"*, and then lists the hardships: trouble, hardship, persecution, famine, nakedness, danger, or sword. The answer is clear: nothing can separate you from God's love. Even when you feel unworthy or unseen, HIS love remains constant.

Paul begins with a question: *"Who shall separate us from the love of Christ?"* Notice he says *who*, pointing to people. No person can separate you from GOD's love. No rejection, no betrayal, no unfollow or silence can undo HIS affection for you.

You are never unloved, no matter who walks away. CHRIST's love holds you when you feel like falling apart. It wipes your tears. It quiets your fears. When no one checks on you, when your phone is silent, when others seem indifferent, HIS love is steadfast. What others think may suggest you're forgotten, but the truth is deeper: CHRIST cares. HIS love is stronger than human love, faithful, present, and unshakable.

Here's how it looks in real time: Marcus lost his job unexpectedly after fifteen years at the company. His coworkers stopped calling. His family didn't know what to say. He felt abandoned and invisible, sitting alone in his living room wondering if anyone cared. But in that quiet, he sensed God reminding him: *"Even here, I love you."* Over time, he found peace in prayer and a new sense of worth, realizing that God's love had never left him, even when people did.

When you stand in front of the mirror, speak it: *"I am never unloved. CHRIST loves me."*

You are not defined by your flaws, failures, or fears. You are held by a love that does not let go, not in distress, destruction, destitution, distraction, or disputes. GOD's love is unconditional and unfailing.

You Are Never Unloved, Mirror Work

Look into the mirror and say aloud:

"I am loved even when I feel unworthy. No rejection, silence, or absence can separate me from Christ's love. His love holds me, sees me, and values me beyond what I can imagine."

Write down the names or situations where you've felt unloved and next to each one write: *"But God still loves me here."*

You Are Never Overcome (Romans 8:35)

Not only are you never unloved, you are never overcome. Paul continues: *"Shall tribulation, distress, persecution, famine, nakedness, peril, or sword?"* He shifts from *who* to *what,* from people to circumstances. You are not defeated by the circumstances that surround you.

Paul lists them: distress, destruction, destitution, distraction, and disputes. Let's break them down with practical examples:

- Not by Distress: When bills pile up and deadlines loom, you feel the pressure, yet you are still standing because God sustains you.

- Not by Destruction: When relationships fall apart and dreams seem to crumble, God keeps you together, holding the pieces of your heart.

- Not by Destitution: When the pantry is bare or the bank account is empty, God provides what you need and reminds you He is your source.

- Not by Distraction: When everyone else's success flashes across your screen and your mind wanders from your purpose, God keeps you focused and reminds you of your own lane.

- Not by Disputes: When conflict rages around you, at work, at home, even in church, His peace anchors you so you don't lose yourself in the chaos.

To the eye it may look like you're losing, but faith tells a different story.

Here's how it looks in real time: Eric was drowning in debt after medical bills piled up. At night he cried, staring at the unpaid notices stacked on his kitchen table. He felt like a failure. Yet somehow, month after month, he kept making it, finding help he didn't expect, learning to budget, watching God provide just enough at the right moment. Though the stress pressed on him, it never crushed him. Looking back, he realized he had endured what he thought he couldn't, and came out stronger.

You Are Never Overcome, Mirror Work

Stand in front of the mirror, take a deep breath, and declare:

"I may feel pressed, but I am not crushed. I may feel tired, but I am not defeated. I am still here, and still standing, because God keeps me."

Then, list one area of your life where you feel overwhelmed, and next to it write what God says about your strength and resilience.

You Are Never Counted Out (Romans 8:36)

Paul writes: "For your sake we are killed all day long; we are accounted as sheep for the slaughter. Yet in all these things we are more than conquerors through Him who loved us."

Every day the enemy punches in to try to destroy you, through temptation, discouragement, fear. Like the Wile E. Coyote who tries every trick to catch the sheep, the enemy plots all day long. And just like in the cartoon, there is a Shepherd, the eternal sheepdog, who keeps watch and blocks every attack.

Maybe you've been laid off and everyone assumes you're finished. Maybe you've been divorced and people treat you like damaged goods. Maybe you've failed publicly, and whispers follow you everywhere. But every time they count you out, God counts you in. Every time they write you off, God writes your name in the Lamb's Book of Life.

Here's what it looks like in real time: After his divorce, Jamal felt like damaged goods. Friends stopped inviting him to gatherings. Even at church, he felt judged and sidelined. People whispered that his ministry was over. But Jamal kept showing up, volunteering quietly, praying, rebuilding himself piece by piece. Years later, God opened doors for him to lead a men's ministry for others walking through brokenness. The same people who counted him out now came to him for advice, and he could finally say: *"I'm still here, still called, still covered."*

You Are Never Counted Out, Mirror Work

Look yourself in the eyes and say:

"They may have written me off, but God wrote me in. Every time they counted me out, God kept me close. I am not finished, my story is still being written."

Write down a moment you thought was your ending, and then note how God brought you through it.

You Are Never on the Level of Others' Expectations (Romans 8:37)

Paul declares, *"No, in all these things we are more than conquerors through him who loved us."* Others may set limits on your life, but God calls you beyond them. You are not confined by their expectations, you exceed them. God has placed greatness in you that surpasses what others imagine.

Paul proclaims: *"In all these things we are more than conquerors."* People may box you in, but God calls you beyond what they expect.

Teachers said you wouldn't succeed. Family doubted your dreams. Colleagues minimized your gifts. But you are not limited by their labels, because you're more than their projections.

Here's how it looks real time: When Ken decided to open his own bakery, everyone doubted him. His parents encouraged him to keep his stable office job. Friends warned him he'd fail. But Ken pushed forward anyway, trusting the vision God gave him. Today, his bakery is thriving, employing others, donating to community events, and even being featured in local media. He surpassed what others expected because he chose to believe what God had placed in his heart over their limited imagination.

You Are Never on the Level of Others' Expectations, Mirror Work

While looking at your reflection, say aloud:

182

"I am not limited by what they expect of me. I am more than their definitions, more than their labels, more than their doubts. I am who God says I am."

Write down a dream or goal others doubted you could reach, and next to it write: *"But God already made a way."*

You Are Never Alone & Never Lonely (Romans 8:38–39)

Paul writes: *"For I am convinced that neither death nor life... will be able to separate us from the love of God."*

You are never alone, not through emotional changes, external forces, existing issues, elevation occurrences, or anything else.

- Through Emotional Changes: When your feelings waver, His presence remains.

- Through External Forces: No outside threat, not the gossip, not the betrayal, can remove you from His hand.

- Through Existing Issues: Even with unresolved struggles, His love is constant.

- Through Elevation Occurrences: Success doesn't push Him away, and failure doesn't disqualify you.

- Through Anything Else: Absolutely nothing, no person, no mistake, no season, can separate you from Him.

Sometimes God even allows loneliness so you can become stationary with the Savior, to focus on Him above all else.

Here's how it looks real time: After moving to a new city, Darryl sat alone in his apartment on Sunday morning, scrolling through old photos of friends back home. He'd never felt lonelier, no texts, no invitations, no familiar faces. But that morning, he decided to visit a small church down the street. A brother welcomed him, sat next to him, and prayed with him. In that moment, Darryl felt God whisper: *"You are seen. You are not alone."* Slowly, he built new connections, and now even mentors other men in their faith journeys.

You Are Never Alone & Never Lonely, Mirror Work

Stand in front of the mirror, place your hand over your heart, and say:

"Even here, I am not alone. Even in silence, I am fully seen. Even when no one else shows up, God remains with me, and I am enough."

Write down a season where you felt alone and then note how you now see God's presence in that moment.

Reflection Questions

- How would you describe your value in light of God's love?

  _____

  _____

  _____

  _____

  _____

- Do you believe the way you see yourself affects the risks you're willing to take?

  _____

  _____

  _____

  _____

  _____

- Do you believe there is more to you than what is visible?

  _____

  _____

  _____

  _____

  _____

- Have frustrating moments ever led you to pull away from God?

_____

_____

_____

_____

_____

- How secure are you knowing God will never stop loving you?

_____

_____

_____

_____

_____

Scripture Meditation
Romans 8:37
"In all these things we are more than conquerors through him who loved us."

Prayer

God, thank You that I am more than what others see. Remind me that nothing can separate me from Your love. Help me stand in the confidence that I am never unloved, never defeated, never alone, and never beyond Your reach. Amen.

Sidebar: 7 Truths to Remember

- You are never unloved.
- You are never overcome.
- You are never counted out.
- You are never limited by others' expectations.
- You are never alone.
- You are never lonely.
- You are never uncovered.

You are more than meets the eye, because of the One who sees it all.

CHAPTER 12

MADE MORE THAN ENOUGH, RESTING IN GOD'S DESIGN

Text: Psalm 139:13–18

Before we open Psalm 139, let's name what this journey has been teaching us: identity is not something you earn, it's something you embody. In earlier chapters, we saw how identity withstands trials, how mirror work dismantles lies, and how God's presence and love remain steady when everything else falls apart.

This chapter invites you deeper, to see yourself not just as resilient in hardship, but as intentionally crafted and fully enough from the very beginning. Identity doesn't just tell you who you are, it reminds you that you are more than meets the eye: never unloved, never overcome, never counted out. Not by distress. Not by destruction. Not by distraction. Not even by death.

Identity is the armor that holds you together when everything else falls apart, and the mirror work you do here helps you see yourself the way God sees you.

We live in a world that tells you you're never enough. When you forget who God created you to be, you chase validation in people, possessions, or performance. You try to earn what God already spoke over you. That's all sin really is, missing the mark of who God already declared you to be.

The enemy knows this too, that's why the serpent in Eden didn't just tempt Eve with fruit; he tempted her with doubt. *"Maybe you're not enough. Maybe God is holding back. Maybe you need to reach beyond yourself to matter."*

But you don't need to become more, you need to remember that you already are more than enough.

Psalm 139 invites you into a deeper kind of mirror work, to stand before the mirror and see not flaws, but craftsmanship. Not inadequacy, but intention. Not shame, but sanctity.

If you've ever wondered, *"Am I enough?"*, this chapter answers clearly: *Yes. You are.*

So what makes you more than enough? Let's discover together.

You Were Personally Constructed

Verse 13 says: *"For you created my inmost being; you knit me together in my mother's womb."*

David reminds us that GOD GOD's self, without consultation or outside input, personally formed your inward parts and covered you in your mother's womb. GOD made you from the inside out, heart, mind, lungs, bones, skin, exactly as GOD envisioned. No angel assisted; no committee decided. GOD thought of you, planned you, and handcrafted you for GOD's purpose.

This wasn't delegated to angels or left to chance. GOD GOD's self, the same GOD who sees all, knows all, and is present everywhere, deliberately formed you in your mother's womb.

Real-life example: You may have grown up feeling unseen because your parents favored your siblings, but GOD designed you with unique creativity and resilience for the calling GOD placed on your life.

When you see yourself in the mirror, you should see the intentional handiwork of the CREATOR, a reflection of GOD's perfect plan. Like GOD told Jeremiah, before GOD formed you, GOD thought about you. You are not accidental or generic, you were personally constructed – every detail, your temperament, your gifts, your appearance, was handcrafted to GOD's specifications, for GOD's assignment.

You Were Personally Constructed, Mirror Work

Stand before the mirror and say:

"Every detail of me, my mind, my heart, my gifts, even my quirks, was personally handcrafted by God. I am not an accident or an afterthought. I am intentionally made, inside and out."

Now, place your hands over your chest and silently thank God for one feature, one trait, and one talent you see in yourself that reflects His handiwork. Write them down.

You Were Perfectly Created

The psalmist declares: *"I praise you because I am fearfully and wonderfully made."*

David moves from acknowledging GOD's handiwork to praising GOD for it. Knowing that GOD personally constructed him fills David with awe. He says, *"I praise you because I am fearfully and wonderfully made. Marvelous are your works."*

When you see yourself through GOD's eyes, you recognize that you are His perfect work. GOD didn't make mistakes when GOD made you. GOD didn't apologize for your uniqueness or regret your design. You are not flawed. You are not a mistake. Every feature of yours reflects GOD's perfect plan. You don't need others' validation, GOD already validated you.

Real-life example: Maybe you've been bullied about your appearance or doubted your worth because of a disability, but GOD calls you marvelous and crafted you perfectly for your purpose.

When you look at yourself, you should see the best of what GOD designed, GOD's intentional handiwork, GOD's masterpiece.

Your awe toward GOD should also extend to how you view yourself, because you are made in GOD's image, the *imago Dei.* You don't have to look at sunsets or mountains to see GOD's glory, just look in the mirror. When you see yourself, you're seeing the intentional, marvelous work of GOD.

You Were Perfectly Created, Mirror Work

Look yourself in the eyes and declare:

"I am fearfully and wonderfully made, marvelous and worth celebrating. Nothing about me is a mistake. I am God's masterpiece."

Then, smile at your reflection, even if it feels awkward, and name out loud one part of yourself (physical or emotional) that you've criticized in the past but now choose to see as marvelous.

You Were Privately Confirmed

Verse 15 reminds us: *"My frame was not hidden from you when I was made in the secret place."*

Here David shows that you were privately confirmed without exception. GOD shaped your frame, the underlying structure that supports everything else, knowing exactly what you could handle. Like a builder who frames a house to bear weight, GOD constructed you in secret, preparing you for the pressures of life.

Only GOD knows how much you can carry because GOD built you that way. That's why you must stay connected to GOD, the One who knows your limits and strengthens you under strain.

Real-life example: That season of battling addiction alone, or silently enduring abuse, felt shameful. But it became the foundation of your testimony, proving GOD's strength in your weakness.

And here's the beautiful part: even the parts of you that feel shameful, that private battle with addiction, that brokenness you hide from the world, GOD shaped you knowing those areas would one day become testimonies of GOD's strength in your weakness. The lowest places, depression, doubt, failure, are where GOD skillfully wrought you, forming resilience and faith that can't be manufactured any other way.

You Were Privately Confirmed, Mirror Work

Breathe deeply, close your eyes for a moment, then look again and say:

"Even in my hidden seasons, the struggles no one saw, the nights I cried alone, God was shaping me. I am stronger because of what He formed in secret."

Think of one private battle you've endured that grew your strength or deepened your faith. Acknowledge it aloud: "That season didn't break me, it built me."

You Were Providentially Consecrated

Verse 16 says: *"Your eyes saw my unformed body; all the days ordained for me were written in your book before one of them came to be."*

You were providentially consecrated, set apart by GOD's wisdom and sovereignty, without erasure, without mistake. The psalmist marvels that GOD saw his substance before it was formed and wrote out all his days in GOD's book. Every moment, every high, every low, every in-between, was included in the divine plan.

When GOD designed you, GOD didn't just draft the highlights. GOD wrote your story fully, the good days, the bad decisions, the heartbreaks, the victories, and called it very good. GOD consecrated you knowing you would stumble, knowing you would question GOD, knowing you would feel inadequate, and yet GOD still gave you purpose.

Real-life examples make this clear:

- That failed business that left you feeling ashamed? GOD already wrote that as a lesson to develop your perseverance and creativity.

- That divorce or breakup that you thought disqualified you? GOD knew it would strengthen your resolve and deepen your dependence on GOD.

- That season of depression where you felt like you were barely holding on? GOD saw it as the soil where resilience and empathy would grow.

Even your omissions, the times you missed the mark, were accounted for. GOD didn't erase you when you fell. Instead, GOD allowed those moments to shape you for what was ahead.

GOD's providence means your path has never been random. GOD blessed you before giving instructions (Genesis 1:28), knowing you would falter but also knowing the lessons learned would lead you closer to GOD.

You Were Providentially Consecrated, Mirror Work

Stand tall and declare:

"My story, the good, the bad, the broken, the beautiful, is already written and redeemed. Every step of my journey has purpose, and nothing is wasted."

Then, write down one setback or painful moment from your past and beside it write what lesson, growth, or testimony came out of it. Say aloud: "God already wrote this into my story and called it good."

You Are Positively Considered

Verse 17 proclaims: *"How precious to me are your thoughts, God! How vast is the sum of them!"*

GOD thinks of you constantly, not with regret but with joy. Not only did GOD create you, but GOD still remembers and considers you every moment.

Real-life example: Being stereotyped at work as "aggressive" or "unapproachable," passed over for opportunities because of others' biases, yet GOD never stops thinking about you with love. Even when your phone is silent and no one seems to notice your sacrifices, GOD sends you new mercy every morning.

We often act out or make risky decisions because we feel forgotten. But when you know that the CREATOR of the universe is thinking about you, carefully, continually, you can rest. You don't need them to remember you if GOD does. Their opinions don't determine your provision, your blessing, or your destiny. GOD doesn't need their approval to open doors for you, to elevate you, or to love on you.

You Are Positively Considered, Mirror Work

Look at your reflection and whisper:

"God thinks of me constantly, not with regret, but with love and delight. Even when I feel forgotten, He sees me, knows me, and provides for me."

List one area of your life where you've felt overlooked or misjudged. Beside it write: "Yet God has never stopped thinking about me here."

You Are Preeminently Covered

Verse 18 concludes: *"When I awake, I am still with you."*

Even when you fail, doubt, or wander, you are still covered. GOD stays. His love wakes with you each morning. You are secure, not because you never falter, but because GOD never lets go.

Real-life example: Waking up in a hospital bed after a bad decision, surviving financial ruin after foreclosure, feeling abandoned after a public fall, and yet still breathing, still covered, still provided for.

Real-life example: Sitting at a funeral for someone you loved but couldn't save, feeling like you failed them, yet still waking up the next day with breath in your body, hope in your heart, and GOD's presence beside you.

You don't need to chase approval through alcohol, drugs, or risky choices. You are already affirmed by the ONE who formed and covers you. You don't have to perform to belong. You don't have to hide your scars or prove your worth. You are already enough because GOD made you so. Every part of you, what's visible and what's hidden, is fearfully and wonderfully made.

This week, stand in front of your mirror every morning, take a deep breath, and declare:

"I am made more than enough, because of the One who made me."

Then go and live like it, with confidence, with joy, and with gratitude for the GOD who constructed, created, confirmed, consecrated, considered, and covers you.

You Are Preeminently Covered, Mirror Work

Take a deep breath, place your hands on your shoulders like a hug, and say:

"No matter how far I've wandered, how many mistakes I've made, or how much I've doubted, God has never let go of me. I wake up every day still covered by His grace and love."

Write down a moment you thought would destroy you, and then next to it, write how God carried you through. Then say aloud: "I am still here, still loved, still covered."

Reflection Questions

- What part of your design have you struggled to accept?

  _____

  _____

  _____

  _____

  _____

- How does knowing you were personally constructed change your self-view?

  _____

  _____

  _____

  _____

  _____

- Where have you seen God's providence even in your mistakes?

  _____

  _____

  _____

  _____

  _____

- How can you rest more in the assurance that you are already enough?

_____

_____

_____

_____

_____

- In what ways have you tried to earn what God already gave you freely?

_____

_____

_____

_____

_____

- What hidden strengths or lessons have emerged from the parts of your story you once wanted to erase?

_____

_____

_____

_____

_____

- How would your daily choices change if you fully believed you are already more than enough?

_____

_____

_____

_____

_____

Scripture Mediation
Psalm 139:14
"I praise you because I am fearfully and wonderfully made; your works are wonderful, I know that full well."

Prayer

GOD, thank You for making me fearfully and wonderfully, with intention and love. Forgive me for doubting Your design and trying to earn what You already gave me freely. Help me to see myself through Your eyes, as chosen, complete, and more than enough. Teach me to let go of false labels and to walk boldly in the truth that nothing can separate me from Your love. Today I rest in the assurance that I am Your masterpiece, covered and called. In Jesus' name, Amen.

Sidebar: 6 Truths to Remember

- You were personally constructed.
- You were perfectly created.

- You were privately confirmed.

- You were providentially consecrated.

- You are positively considered.

- You are preeminently covered.

Stand before the mirror and declare: "I am made more than enough, because of the One who made me."

CHAPTER 13

I AM WHO GOD SAYS I AM, STANDING IN YOUR ASSIGNMENT

Text: Jeremiah 1:4–10

We've learned how identity sustains us through trials, how mirror work dismantles lies, and how to embrace our worth in the eyes of God. But knowing you are made more than enough is not just about being, it's about doing. It's about standing confidently in the assignment God has written into your DNA.

The enemy's greatest weapon is to convince you you're disqualified, too flawed, too young, too broken. But the truth is: you are exactly who God says you are. You are not who they named you. You are not who your failures suggest. You are not even the sum of what you see in the mirror, you are who God calls you.

At this stage in your journey of reformation and mirror work, it's time to confront one of the deepest truths about identity: you are not who they say you are, you are exactly who God says you are.

You're not the sum of their labels, not the weight of their rejection, not the echo of their expectations. You are not what your critics called you, nor what your circumstances tried to reduce you to. You are not just your mistakes or even your achievements. You are, wholly, fully, who God says you are.

This is vital to understand because once you embrace who God says you are, you stop living for other people's validation. You stop shrinking to fit into their boxes. You stop editing yourself just to make them comfortable.

When you really know who God says you are, you realize you don't need to audition for approval. You don't need to perform for applause. God's word over your life is final, and enough.

In Jeremiah 1, we witness Jeremiah wrestling with his own insecurities. God calls him, affirms him, and assigns him, yet Jeremiah protests: "But I'm too young... I can't speak... I'm not enough."

Sound familiar? How many times have you looked in the mirror and doubted what you saw because of what they said, or because of what fear said? But here's the good news: God interrupts Jeremiah's excuses and says, "Do not say that... because I knew you before you even knew yourself. I've already set you apart. I've already assigned you. And I will be with you."

This chapter builds on everything we've uncovered so far:

Mirror work that exposes the lies and reflects the truth.

Reclaiming your worth and rejecting false labels.

Standing confidently in your divine design.

Now it's time to step into the next level, embracing your assignment and living boldly in who God says you are.

What happens when you fully accept that you are who God says you are, and nothing less?

What does it mean to stand in that identity and fulfill your assignment?

Let's work through what God said to Jeremiah, and what He still says to you today.

Your Poor Formation Doesn't Stop God's Faithfulness

The first lesson in understanding what it means to be who God says you are is this: your poor formation does not disqualify you from God's faithfulness.

When God called Jeremiah, the prophet immediately began making excuses: "Ah, Lord God, I cannot speak, for I am a youth!" He knew the language of faith, he even addressed God as Sovereign Lord, yet he didn't believe God could actually use him.

Why? Because Jeremiah's formation, his upbringing, teaching, and experiences, had trained him to believe more in his flaws than in God's faithfulness.

Verse 1 reveals that Jeremiah came from a priestly lineage. His father, Hilkiah, was a priest in Anathoth. That should have given him confidence, a spiritual head start. But somewhere along the way, despite growing up in a "holy household," Jeremiah internalized the wrong message: that his youth, his limitations, and his inadequacies disqualified him.

How many of us have been there?

- Raised in church yet convinced God only uses "perfect people."

- Taught all the right words but feeling too dirty, too unworthy, too broken to be chosen.

- Sitting under sermons but secretly believing the promises applied to everyone but you.

We've been formed to think God's faithfulness has limits. But Jeremiah's story reminds us: God's call overrides our formation. His faithfulness is bigger than our upbringing, our doubts, and our brokenness.

Real-world examples:

✅ A man raised in a rigid religious tradition who was told his anger and his questions made him unfit, yet God used his boldness to become an advocate for justice.

✅ A young woman who grew up in a fractured home and believed love was conditional, yet God called her to mentor and mother others with grace.

✅ A man taught that his disability was a punishment, yet God gave him a platform to inspire millions through his perseverance and faith.

You may have been taught to believe that your youth, your mistakes, your insecurities, or even your body disqualify you, but God sees beyond that.

Your poor formation, flawed theology, unhealthy family patterns, cultural expectations, does not cancel out God's faithfulness.

When you stand in the mirror and confront the lies you inherited, that you're too messed up, too inexperienced, too broken, speak this truth to yourself:

My poor formation doesn't stop His faithfulness. I am still who God says I am."

Mirror Work: Your Poor Formation Doesn't Stop God's Faithfulness

Stand in the mirror, lock eyes with yourself, and speak this aloud:

"Everything that shaped me, the good, the bad, the flawed, does not disqualify me. My broken places don't block His blessing. My history does not cancel His faithfulness. I am still chosen. I am still His."

Write down 2–3 lies your upbringing or experiences taught you about yourself (e.g., "I'm too broken," "I'm not enough"), then cross them out and write next to each: "But God says: I am His. I am who He says I am."

Your Confirmation Comes Without Co-Signers

The first truth we learned is that your poor formation doesn't stop God's faithfulness. But here's the second:

When you are who God says you are, your confirmation comes without any co-signers.

Look at what the text says in Jeremiah 1:4, "Then the word of the Lord came to me…"

God spoke directly to Jeremiah.

Not through Michael or Gabriel. Not through a prophet or a priest. Not through a council, a vote, or even his own father (who was a priest).

This is critical: when God declares who you are, you don't need anyone else's permission or validation to believe it and walk in it.

God didn't gather a committee to affirm Jeremiah's calling.

God didn't consult a board or call a family meeting.

He spoke directly to Jeremiah, and that was enough.

Real-World Examples:

✅ A young Black woman hears God call her to preach, but her church board votes "no", yet she still starts ministering in shelters, on corners, and online because God already said "yes."

✅ A man feels called to start a business that honors God and serves his community, but his family mocks him, saying he'll fail, yet he trusts God's confirmation and launches anyway.

✅ Someone senses God calling them to break generational curses, to forgive, to parent differently, but others in the family roll their eyes or dismiss it, yet they press forward because God already confirmed it in their spirit.

How many times have you delayed moving because you were waiting for others to validate what God already spoke?

How many times have you heard from God and then posted it on Facebook hoping for likes?

Or called your cousin, your mentor, your pastor, asking: "Do you think this is really God?"

The truth is: you don't need a co-signer when God Himself has already signed your name.

When God calls you, it doesn't matter who doesn't clap, who doesn't comment, who doesn't show up. His confirmation is enough.

He comes to you directly because He created you uniquely.

Mirror Work: Your Confirmation Comes Without Co-Signers

Stand tall, shoulders back, and tell yourself:

"I don't need a committee. I don't need a crowd. I don't need anyone else to approve me because God already did. His word over me is final. His voice is enough."

Then, silently thank God for one area of your life where He's already spoken clearly, even if others didn't believe in you, and say aloud:

"I agree with what God has spoken over me, no co-signers required."

Your Design Was Deliberate

Here's the third truth:

My design was deliberate.

God said to Jeremiah, and to you:

"Before I formed you in the womb, I knew you."

Say that slowly:

"Before I formed you."

God was saying your design wasn't random, accidental, or flawed. It wasn't the result of chance or circumstance.

Before genetics, before your parents even met, God formed you.

So before you get angry about the things you don't like about yourself, before you question your skin tone, your hair texture, your nose, your height, your voice, remember: God formed you.

He made you on purpose, with intention, Himself.

And yet how often do we, as Black men, feel pressured to dislike what God designed? To shrink because of how society perceives us?

God says:

"That rich, dark skin? My idea. That broad nose? My artistry. Those full lips? My design. That baritone voice? My handiwork. I didn't mess up. I formed you deliberately."

Real-World Examples for Black Men:

☑ A young Black man is teased about his dark skin growing up, internalizing colorism, but later stands proud, realizing his hue reflects the richness of his people and the Creator's brilliance.

☑ Another grows up ashamed of his coarse, tightly-coiled hair after years of being told it was "unprofessional", but eventually wears it with pride, knowing it crowns him with history and strength.

☑ A man resents his broad shoulders and imposing build, believing it makes him a target or stereotype, but learns to use his presence to protect, inspire, and lead.

☑ A brother grows frustrated with his deep voice because it draws unwanted assumptions of anger or aggression, but discovers that same voice commands respect and carries truth.

☑ Another despises his facial features, his wide nose, his strong jaw, until he realizes those same features connect him to ancestors who endured, resisted, and thrived.

We waste so much time wishing we looked like someone else, trying to fit into standards that were never meant for us. But all along, God has been waiting for us to embrace the masterpiece He made.

Stop trying to "fix" what society told you was broken. Stop reshaping yourself to fit in rooms you were meant to transform.

Be the best steward of the you God made.

Mirror Work: Your Design Was Deliberate

Look at your features, your skin, your eyes, your hair, your hands, and say to each:

"You are not a mistake. You were crafted on purpose. My Creator made me fearfully and wonderfully, with intention and care. I embrace every part of myself as His masterpiece."

Write down the one feature, trait, or characteristic you've criticized the most, and next to it write: "This too was God's idea, and it is good."

Your Preparation Was Painstaking

Here's the fourth truth:

A lot of planning and preparation went into my person.

God tells Jeremiah:

"Before I formed you in the womb, I knew you."

That word knew in the Hebrew implies a deep, intentional, conscious effort. It means God didn't just throw you together; He thought you through. He envisioned every detail before forming you, every trait, every feature, every temperament, every gift.

"I spent time planning and preparing the being that was going to be formed in the womb," God says.

"Even in choosing the womb you were placed in, I chose two people who would contribute exactly the traits I wanted for you. I gave you your mother's determination and your father's charisma. I gave you your grandmother's wisdom and your grandfather's creativity. I designed the way your shoulders would square when you stood tall, the way your eyes would glint when you smiled, the way your laugh would linger in a room. I thought of all that before you ever breathed."

This is not random. You're not just a product of biology, you are the result of God's painstaking preparation.

Real-World Examples for Black Men:

✅ The brother who inherited his mother's fiery advocacy and his father's smooth diplomacy, enabling him to speak up for justice yet maintain peace.

✅ The young man whose broad nose and deep voice drew teasing in school, but years later became the very traits that earned him respect in boardrooms and pulpits.

✅ The father who grew up poor but was equipped by God with both hustle and compassion, allowing him to break generational cycles and model love for his sons.

✅ The artist whose sensitivity to pain and sharp eye for beauty, traits passed down through generations, now allow him to create work that heals his community.

✅ The brother in leadership who sometimes doubts himself, but realizes God crafted his quiet confidence and ability to listen to uplift others more powerfully than words ever could.

Even the struggles and quirks you inherited have a place. What you thought was a flaw, a quick temper, an emotional depth, a stoic demeanor, was part of God's blueprint, meant to be refined and used for His glory.

You are not a prototype, nor a mistake, nor an afterthought.

You are the exact being God envisioned when He said, "Let there be you."

Mirror Work: Your Preparation Was Painstaking

Pause in front of the mirror and say:

"I was worth the time. God thought me through. My gifts, my temperament, even my quirks, all planned and prepared before I ever took a breath. I am exactly who I was meant to be."

Take a few moments to write down 2–3 ways God uniquely prepared you for the season you're in now, traits or experiences that equip you to do what others can't.

Your Positioning Was Purposeful

Here's the fifth truth:

My positioning was purposeful.

God tells Jeremiah:

"Before I formed you in the womb, I knew you. Before you were born, I sanctified you."

That word sanctified means set apart. In other words, God was intentional about where and how you entered the world. Even if the story you were told about your childhood sounded chaotic, unstable, or unwanted, none of it was random.

God planted you in the exact soil that would grow you into who you were meant to become.

Maybe you were raised by your grandmother instead of your mother. Maybe your father was absent, or your family struggled with poverty. Maybe you felt like everyone else got more love, more freedom, or more opportunity. But the truth is:

God knew what it would take to develop you.

God knew what kind of dirt would strengthen your roots.

God knew what kind of discomfort would drive you toward your destiny.

Even the painful parts of your upbringing were purposeful.

Real-World Examples for Black Men:

✅ The brother who grew up in a public housing project surrounded by crime but learned resilience and leadership, now running programs for youth who grew up just like him.

✅ The young man who bounced between relatives after his mother was incarcerated, who developed deep empathy for broken families and became a mentor and counselor.

✅ The boy who was the "quiet one" in a loud, boisterous household, who grew up learning how to listen, discern, and lead with wisdom in tense spaces.

✅ The man who was always told to "stay on the porch" while others ran the streets, who now owns the house and the block because his discipline was cultivated early.

✅ The brother who grew up with tough-love parents and envied his friends' more permissive homes, only to realize later that their strictness shaped him into someone trustworthy, responsible, and respected.

Some of us were planted in lush gardens.

Some of us were roses that pushed through concrete.

Either way, the flower still bloomed, and the fruit still grew.

Your origin doesn't have to be glamorous to be glorious.

God chose the soil where you'd flourish.

Mirror Work: Your Positioning Was Purposeful

Sit or stand and look at yourself as you say:

"Where I came from was not random. My story, every chapter, was written with care. God planted me exactly where I needed to be to grow into who I am. My roots matter. My soil matters. I was positioned on purpose."

Write one sentence about your upbringing or environment that you've always resented or questioned, and then write beneath it: "God used this to grow me."

Your Assignment Is Appointed

Not only is your position purposeful, but the assignment tied to your position is appointed by God.

God says to Jeremiah:

"Before you were born, I sanctified you; I ordained you a prophet to the nations."

Notice the sequence: Before He formed you, He already knew you. Before you took your first breath, He already set you apart. Which means, where you are right now is not an accident.

This ties directly to what we studied in Psalm 139 last chapter: you were providentially consecrated, your days written out before you lived even one.

Where you stand today, even if it feels like a wilderness, is part of God's appointed plan for your life.

Real-World Examples:

✅ A Black man working a warehouse job while others climb corporate ladders, but God positioned him there to become the steady presence and mentor young men around him needed, showing integrity in an environment that lacks it.

✅ A Black woman raising children as a single mother while her peers travel the world, yet her assignment is to raise a generation of kids who know resilience, faith, and love.

✅ A brother passed over for a promotion, but appointed where he is to build a business on the side that will bless his whole community.

✅ A sister working at a local school instead of a "prestigious" university, because she's been placed where young girls need to see what leadership, grace, and brilliance look like in a woman who looks like them.

The Comparison Trap:

So many of us spend hours scrolling social media, comparing our "here" to someone else's "there."

We covet their cars, their careers, their captions, but miss that our blessing is waiting where we already stand.

If Elijah had stopped 13 miles short of Cherith because the ocean looked better than the brook, he would've starved, because his blessing was tied to his obedience.

You can't catch your blessing at their destination.

You can't reap their harvest.

You can't live their story, and still expect to receive what God wrote into yours.

Where you are is where God intended.

Your "here" has a purpose.

Your season has an assignment.

Mirror Work: Your Assignment Is Appointed

Take a deep breath and speak this boldly to your reflection:

"My assignment is mine. It was appointed to me before I was born. I don't need to compare or compete, I just need to complete it. I am exactly where I need to be to do what God called me to do."

List 1–2 steps you can take this week to walk toward your assignment, however small, and pray over them: "Bless my obedience, God."

Your Excuses Don't Erase God's Expectation

Jeremiah, like so many of us, tried to disqualify himself.

"Alas, Lord God! Behold, I cannot speak, for I am a youth." (Jeremiah 1:6)

But God responded:

"Do not say, 'I am a youth,' for you shall go to all to whom I send you, and whatever I command you, you shall speak."

God heard the excuse, and immediately crushed it.

That's because excuses don't erase expectations.

They don't lower the bar.

They don't cancel the assignment.

When God calls you, He already accounted for your weaknesses, your fears, your flaws, and still said: You're the one for this.

Real-World Examples:

✅ A Black man who says, "Lord, I can't lead this ministry, I've been incarcerated." But God already planned to use his testimony to reach others in the same situation.

✅ A Black woman who says, "Lord, I can't start this business, I don't have a degree." But God already gave her creativity, resilience, and connections that no classroom could provide.

✅ A young brother saying, "I'm too young; they won't listen." But God appoints him to mentor his peers through spoken word and lived example.

☑ A sister saying, "I've made too many mistakes, I don't deserve to be used." But God says: It's because of those mistakes that you'll speak with authenticity and power to those still in the pit.

Excuses are really just idols we build to avoid the discomfort of obedience.

We think our insecurity trumps God's sovereignty.

But the same God who appointed you has already equipped you, even if you can't see it yet.

Mirror Work: Your Excuses Don't Erase God's Expectation

Look at yourself firmly and say:

"My fears don't disqualify me. My mistakes don't disqualify me. My excuses don't diminish His expectation. He called me knowing all of this, and still chose me. I will rise and go."

Write down your top excuse or fear, then draw a line through it and replace it with: "But God says: Go."

God's Assurance Conquers Your Apprehension

"Do not be afraid of their faces, for I am with you to deliver you," says the Lord. (Jeremiah 1:8)

This is the final word in this text, and it's the one that ties everything together.

When you are who God says you are, His assurance becomes the antidote to your apprehension.

Notice: Jeremiah never said what he was afraid of, but God already knew.

God told him, "Don't be afraid. You walk in your assignment, and I'll walk with you. If their faces intimidate you, don't worry, I'm right there. If the money doesn't add up, I'll provide. If the plan seems unclear, trust that I already know the plans I have for you."

God's assurance tells you: If I gave you the assignment, I'm also responsible for clearing the way for its completion.

Real-World Examples:

✅ A young Black man stepping into a corporate boardroom full of people who doubt him, yet God whispers, "Don't be afraid of their faces. I'm with you."

✅ A Black woman launching a nonprofit in a community that dismisses her, yet God reassures, "You'll say what I tell you to say, and I'll handle the resistance."

✅ A brother preaching his first sermon in a congregation that's skeptical, and he remembers, "I am with you to deliver you."

✅ A sister walking into family court, feeling overwhelmed, but knowing God has already gone ahead of her to fight her battle.

Application:

Your apprehension may take the form of fear, doubt, intimidation, insecurity, or simply not knowing what's next.

But if God called you, God covers you.

If God formed you, God fights for you.

If God appointed you, God assures you.

All you have to do is keep walking.

You don't have to figure it all out, you just have to follow.

And here's the beauty: the very things you thought would stop you, the intimidating faces, the closed doors, the lack of resources, become the stage where God's faithfulness shines brightest.

So stop letting fear keep you still.

Stop letting apprehension outweigh your assignment.

Walk boldly. You're not alone.

Walk confidently. You're not uncovered.

Walk fully, because God's assurance conquers everything you're afraid to face.

Mirror Work: God's Assurance Conquers Your Apprehension

Rest your hands on your chest and say softly but confidently:

"God is with me. His presence walks with me into every room, every battle, every assignment. I do not have to be afraid. His assurance cancels my apprehension."

Then close your eyes and breathe slowly, saying: "I trust You. Lead me. I will not fear their faces."

Reflection Questions:

- What excuses have you been using to delay walking in your assignment?

_____

_____

_____

_____

_____

- What "faces" have you been afraid of, and how might God be calling you to look past them?

_____

_____

_____

_____

_____

- How have I allowed others' opinions to overshadow what God has already spoken about me?

_____

_____

_____

_____

_____

- In what areas of my life am I still waiting for "permission" to step into what God has already confirmed?

_____

_____

_____

_____

_____

- What specific step can I take this week to walk more boldly in my God-given assignment?

_____

_____

_____

_____

_____

- How does knowing God planned you in detail before you were born change your confidence today?

_____

_____

_____

_____

_____

- Where in your life do you need to take the next step without fear?

_____

_____

_____

_____

_____

Scripture Meditation
Ephesians 2:10 (NLT)
"For we are God's masterpiece. He has created us anew in Christ Jesus, so we can do the good things he planned for us long ago."

Prayer:

God, thank You for knowing me before I was formed and calling me anyway. Thank You for seeing past my flaws and failures and appointing me for Your purposes. Forgive me for letting fear, excuses, and doubt stand in the way. Today, I choose to trust You. Help me to walk boldly into the assignment You've given me, confident that You're with me, covering me, and clearing the way. In Jesus' name, Amen.

Sidebar: 6 Truths to Remember

☑ Your poor formation doesn't stop His faithfulness.

☑ Your confirmation comes without co-signers.

☑ Your design was deliberate.

- [x] Your preparation was painstaking.
- [x] Your positioning was purposeful.
- [x] God's assurance conquers your apprehension.

CHAPTER 14

I HAVE NOTHING TO PROVE, STANDING FIRM IN WHO GOD SAYS I AM

Text: Matthew 4:1–11

We've reached the final mirror.

In this book, we've journeyed through the wilderness of our own reflection, confronting lies, dismantling false labels, and reclaiming the truth of who God says we are. We've learned to see ourselves rightly: personally constructed, perfectly created, privately confirmed, providentially consecrated, positively considered, and preeminently covered.

We've confronted our flawed formation, shed our excuses, stood boldly in our deliberate design, and claimed the confidence to walk in our appointed assignments. We've stared into the mirror and begun to believe what God sees.

But identity, as we've said all along, is not just a concept. Identity is not just an image in your head or a word you write on paper. Identity is only image until it's tested.

That's what this final chapter is about.

Jesus models it for us in Matthew 4. The text says:

"Then Jesus was led up by the Spirit into the wilderness to be tempted by the devil. And when he had fasted forty days and forty nights, afterward he was hungry. Now when the tempter came to him, he said, 'If you are the Son of God...'"

The enemy's strategy is clear: to make you question what God has already declared.

Right before this moment, at His baptism, Jesus heard the Father say publicly:

"This is my beloved Son, in whom I am well pleased."

And now the devil shows up, not to attack His body but His identity.

"If you are the Son of God..."

That's what temptation is really about. Not just your willpower. Not just your behavior. But whether you will stand firm in who God says you already are.

The wilderness is not about proving yourself to people, because they'll believe what they want anyway. It's not even about proving yourself to yourself.

The wilderness is where you prove to God: I am who You said I am.

And here's the good news, the message of this final chapter:

You don't have to perform.

You don't have to panic.

You don't have to prove.

You already are who He says you are, even when tested.

The enemy wants you to disappoint God. But God allows the wilderness to draw out of you the best He already put in you.

So as we close this series of mirror work and reformation, take one last deep breath and declare:

"I have nothing to prove. Not to them. Not to the enemy. Not even to myself. I am who God says I am."

Let's walk through this wilderness together and see how to stand firm, even when everything and everyone tries to make you doubt.

Your Current Condition Doesn't Change God's Confirmation

When you truly grasp that you have nothing to prove, the first thing you need to embrace is this:

Your current condition does not change His confirmation.

Look at the text. Matthew 4 says:

"Then Jesus was led by the Spirit into the wilderness to be tempted… and after fasting forty days and forty nights, he was hungry."

Jesus is physically weak. His body is tired. His stomach is empty. His strength is spent. His condition screams vulnerability, yet even here, His Father's words still stand:

"This is my beloved Son, in whom I am well pleased."

Even when you're hungry, you're still His child.

Even when you're weak, you're still chosen.

Even when you're broke, lonely, or grieving, you're still His beloved.

Real-World Examples:

- A Black man working two jobs to feed his family, yet still feeling inadequate because society measures him by wealth or status. Even when his wallet is empty, God still calls him "My son."

- A young Black woman balancing motherhood and college, feeling judged because of her struggles, but God still calls her "My daughter, in whom I delight."

- A brother returning from incarceration, labeled by his past, but God still calls him "Beloved, redeemed, and chosen."

- A sister battling depression and feeling invisible, yet God still whispers: "You are mine."

We live in a culture where people withdraw love and respect when your condition changes. Lose your job? They stop calling. Get sick? They disappear. Struggle emotionally? They say you're weak.

When you're secure in who God called you to be, you can stop chasing fickle people for approval. If they unfollow, fine. If they gossip, fine. You don't need their applause to walk in your assignment.

So either block them and bloom in peace, or let them watch you blossom without their blessing. Either way, you don't need them.

You don't have to prove anything to anyone. Because even in your weakest moment, God still looks at you and says:

"That's my child. I'm still well pleased."

Mirror Work: Your Current Condition Doesn't Change God's Confirmation

Rest your hands on your chest and say softly but confidently:

"Even here, tired, hungry, hurting, I am still His. My condition does not cancel His confirmation. I am chosen. I am loved. I belong to Him."

Then close your eyes and breathe slowly, saying: "I am still who You say I am."

You Don't Have to Convince Anyone You're Capable

Here's the second truth:

When you know you have nothing to prove, you don't have to convince anyone that you're capable.

Look at the text:

"The tempter came to Him and said, 'If you are the Son of God, command these stones to become bread.' But Jesus answered, 'It is written: Man shall not live by bread alone, but by every word that proceeds from the mouth of God.'"

The enemy begins, "If you are…" but a better translation would be, "Since you are…"

That's key, because the tempter already knows who Jesus is.

Temptation is always personal.

It knows who you are before it even comes to your door.

Temptation doesn't show up confused, it comes informed.

It's not asking because it doubts your ability; it's asking because it wants you to misuse your ability.

Real-World Examples:

- As a Black man in the workplace, someone tries to provoke you by questioning your intelligence or leadership, but deep down they already know you're capable, they just want you to lose your composure and "prove it."

- As a Black woman, a colleague might imply you're "too ambitious" or "aggressive," but it's really because they recognize your gifts and feel threatened, they know you're more than capable already.

- You're a father under financial strain, and the temptation comes to cut corners or compromise your integrity to provide, but it's not because you're incapable, it's because you are capable, and the enemy hopes you'll use your strength the wrong way.

- You're a single mother tempted to settle for unhealthy relationships just to prove you're desirable, but you don't have to.

Temptation always comes crafted to your specific capabilities. It's not trying to convince itself of what you can do, it already knows. The real battle is whether you believe you have nothing to prove.

When you have nothing to prove, you can stand in the middle of the test and simply say, "Man shall not live by bread alone."

You can walk away from the argument, ignore the bait, and save your energy, because you don't owe anyone a demonstration of your power.

You don't have to turn stones into bread.

You don't have to buy the shoes to show you can afford them.

You don't have to clap back to prove you're smart enough.

You don't have to settle just to show you're wanted.

When you know who you are, you can let temptation watch you stay true to who God says you are, and that's more powerful than proving anything.

Mirror Work: You Don't Have to Convince Anyone You're Capable

Stand tall, shoulders back, and say firmly:

"I don't have to prove my worth. My strength speaks for itself. God has already declared me capable, and I choose to honor Him, not their doubts."

Then close your eyes and breathe slowly, saying: "I trust who You made me to be."

You Don't Allow Others to Command What You Control

When you know you have nothing to prove, here's the third truth:

I don't allow you to command what I control.

Look at what happens in the text:

"Then the devil took Jesus to the holy city, set Him on the pinnacle of the temple, and said, 'If you are the Son of God, throw yourself down. For it is written: He shall give His angels charge over you.'"

Notice this: Satan tried to command Jesus' body to act against Him. But Jesus didn't move.

Why?

Because when you're secure in your identity, no one else can make you act out of character.

Real-World Examples:

- As a Black man, being stopped and provoked by law enforcement who are hoping to escalate a situation. You choose calm, you don't let them command what you control.

- As a Black woman in a workplace meeting, someone questions your expertise, subtly insulting you to trigger a reaction, but you respond with grace and facts, not fury.

- On social media, someone trolls your posts, trying to bait you into an online argument. But you simply delete, block, or disengage because you refuse to let them dictate your behavior.

- Family members press your buttons at gatherings, bringing up old wounds, expecting you to lash out, but you remain composed because you know who you are.

Too many of us fall into temptation because we allow others to push us into decisions and actions that betray our identity.

Temptation often comes disguised as pressure, to act quickly, speak harshly, spend recklessly, or compromise integrity, but the power lies in your refusal.

Jesus shows us two powerful practices here:

Prayer Life: Private prayer leads to public power. Even though Jesus was physically weak, His spiritual strength held firm.

Scripture Knowledge: When Satan misquoted Scripture, Jesus was able to correct him confidently because He knew the Word.

When you know who you are and stay rooted in prayer and Word, you refuse to let people misuse Scripture, misrepresent you, or manipulate you into moving.

When you have nothing to prove, you can stay seated in your strength and silence those who try to provoke you.

You can look the tempter in the face, at work, at home, in your own mind, and say, "You don't control me. You don't get to command me. I belong to God."

Mirror Work: You Don't Allow Others to Command What You Control

Place your hands over your heart and say steadily:

"No one can provoke me into acting out of character. I own my choices, my words, my power. I stay steady because I know who I am."

Then close your eyes and breathe slowly, saying: "I remain grounded in You."

You Will Not Be Coerced Into Coveting

When you have nothing to prove, you refuse to let the enemy convince you to crave what was never meant for you.

Look at what happens next. Satan takes Jesus to an exceedingly high mountain, shows Him all the kingdoms of the world and their glory, and says:

"All these things I will give you if you fall down and worship me."

Notice: this time, Satan does not say, "Since you are the Son of God." Why? Because Satan already knows who Jesus is, but he's trying to distract Jesus into wanting more than what God already assigned Him.

That's the trick of temptation, to get you daydreaming about somebody else's assignment while neglecting your own.

Remember, Jesus was led by the Spirit into the wilderness. Where He was, in hunger, in testing, in obscurity, was exactly where God wanted Him at that moment.

And here's the truth: Temptation often shows up to guide you off the path God has for you by making someone else's blessing look better than yours.

Real-World Examples:

- You're grinding at your small business, but every time you scroll Instagram, you see somebody "living the dream" in luxury, and it makes you question if you're enough.

- You're faithfully serving your church or community while another person is getting the spotlight and recognition, and you start to think maybe God forgot about you.

- You're raising your kids with all you have, but you see people flaunting vacations, expensive shoes, and brand-new cars, and you feel inadequate in your own home.

The reality is, you don't know what it cost them to get it, and what they paid for it may not even be a price you're willing or ordained to pay.

Satan was trying to get Jesus to fantasize about a throne without a cross. But if Jesus had taken the bait, none of us would have been saved.

Be careful about those voices, even your own thoughts, that whisper, "This could all be yours," when it's not what God assigned to you.

Faithfulness in the valley is better than fantasy on the mountaintop if the mountaintop is not in God's plan for your life.

What God has for you is yours, no manipulation, no shortcuts, no compromise required.

Stay faithful where you are, and watch God bless you right where He planted you.

Mirror Work: You Will Not Be Coerced Into Coveting

Open your hands in front of you and say with gratitude:

"I release comparison. I bless what others have without craving it. What You have for me is already mine, and I trust Your timing."

Then close your eyes and breathe slowly, saying: "I stay faithful in my own lane."

You Can Call Out Temptation for What It Is

When you truly have nothing to prove, you stop being polite with what's trying to destroy you, and you call it out for what it is.

Look at how Jesus responds at this point in the text.

After enduring temptation after temptation, Jesus finally declares:

"Away with you, Satan!" or in other translations, "Get thee behind me!"

Until now, Jesus has simply countered Satan's offers with scripture, calm, resolute, but patient. But at this moment, Jesus stops entertaining the conversation. He refuses to keep debating. He names the enemy for what he is, not just "the tempter," but Satan, Diablos, the accuser.

At some point, you too have to stop dancing around temptation, stop pretending it's harmless, and recognize it for what it really is: a strategic, targeted attempt to discredit you in front of your Father.

Sometimes you need to say it out loud: "I see you for what you are, and I reject you completely."

Real-World Examples

- You're a Black man at work, and every time you succeed, someone subtly suggests you "got lucky" or "played the race card." Instead of internalizing it or over-explaining yourself, you name it for what it is: an attack meant to shrink you and silence your excellence.

- You're a Black woman in ministry, and someone continually questions whether you're "called", not because of your gifting but because of their bias. Instead of trying to prove yourself, you boldly call it what it is: a spirit of intimidation and insecurity projected onto you.

- You've been faithfully trying to live right, but that ex slides into your DMs late at night with "just checking on you" energy. You don't pretend it's innocent. You block it and say (to yourself and God), "That's a trap, not a friend."

At this point in the wilderness, Jesus shows us something crucial:

You don't owe politeness to what's trying to kill you. You don't have to keep the conversation going. You don't have to smile at what undermines your character. You can, and must, speak with authority and shut it down.

Stop calling it "just a challenge" when it's actually a coordinated attack. Call it the spirit of manipulation. Call it the spirit of envy. Call it out, and tell it to go.

Mirror Work: You Can Call Out Temptation for What It Is

Clench your fists at your sides, look yourself in the eyes, and say boldly:

"I see you, temptation. I name you, and you have no power here. I reject you fully because I belong to God."

Then close your eyes and breathe slowly, saying: "Get behind me. I walk in freedom."

You Can Count on God to Counter the Attacks

When you have nothing to prove, you can rest in this truth: God Himself will step in to counter the attacks that come your way.

Look at the text, verse 11. After all the temptations, the text says:

"Then the devil left him. And behold, angels came and ministered to him."

Don't miss this:

Jesus was physically exhausted, emotionally drained, and spiritually tested to the core. He had fasted for 40 days. He had faced the devil toe-to-toe. He had rejected every lie and temptation hurled his way. And then, just when it seemed like He couldn't take another step, God sent reinforcements.

The angels came, ministered to Him, and restored His strength.

Real-World Examples

- You've been working hard to stay clean from addiction, and you feel like no one notices how hard it is to say no every day. But then a phone call comes, a friend checks in, someone sends a kind word, a door to counseling opens, that's God sending "angels" to minister to you.

- You've been overlooked at work again and again, and you wanted to quit. But the next day, a coworker commends you privately for your integrity, and HR emails you about a new opportunity, that's God countering the attack of discouragement with affirmation.

- You've been fighting a battle in your mind, telling yourself you're not good enough, that no one cares. Then, out of nowhere, a scripture pops into your heart or a sermon speaks directly to your situation, that's God showing up right on time.

God sees the attacks. God honors your endurance. And just when you think you can't stand another minute, He steps in to refresh you, heal you, and hold you steady.

When you know who you are and when you stop trying to prove yourself to people, you discover this: You don't have to fight every battle alone. You don't even have to win in your own strength. If you can stand firm, if you can keep saying "no" to the lies and "yes" to who God says you are, He will take care of the rest.

The enemy will flee, and God will send His presence, through people, through peace, through provision, to remind you: You are never alone. You are never abandoned. You are always covered.

Mirror Work: You Can Count on God to Counter the Attacks

Place both hands over your heart and whisper with assurance:

"God is fighting for me. His angels are with me. Every attack is already being handled. I trust Him to refresh and restore me."

Then close your eyes and breathe slowly, saying: "You are my refuge and strength."

Reflection Questions

- In what ways have you seen God sustain you during your weakest seasons?

_____

_____

_____

_____

_____

- What are some areas where you've been trying to prove yourself to people instead of walking in who God already says you are?

_____

_____

_____

_____

_____

- How does knowing God will fight your battles and send help change how you face temptation and trials?

_____

_____

_____

_____

_____

- Where do you still need to trust God's timing and plan instead of coveting what others have?

_____

_____

_____

_____

_____

- What is one thing you've learned in this book that you will carry into your daily life to remind you of your God-given identity?

_____

_____

_____

_____

_____

Sidebar: 6 Truths to Take With You

- Your current condition does not change God's confirmation.
- You don't have to convince anyone you're capable, you already are.
- You don't allow others to command what you control.

237

- You will not be coerced into coveting what isn't yours.

- You can call out temptation and lies for what they are.

- You can count on God to counter every attack and restore you.

"I am who God says I am, nothing more, nothing less, and nothing else."

Scripture Meditation
Matthew 4:11
"Then the devil left him, and behold, angels came and ministered to him."

Exodus 14:14
"The Lord will fight for you; you need only to be still."

Closing Prayer

God, thank You for walking with me through this journey of identity, healing, and reformation. Thank You for reminding me that I have nothing to prove, not to the world, not to my critics, not even to myself. You have already called me, formed me, set me apart, and confirmed me as Yours.

When I feel weak, help me remember that Your strength is made perfect in my weakness. When temptation comes, help me see it for what it is and stand firm in who You've made me to be. When I'm tempted to covet or compare, remind me of Your perfect plan and provision for my life.

Today, I stand in front of the mirror and boldly declare:

"I am enough, I am chosen, I am covered, because I am who You say I am."

Amen.

Look in the mirror and declare: "I have nothing to prove, I already am who God says I am."

Final Charge: A Benediction

You've looked in the mirror. You've confronted the lies, reclaimed the truth, and stood tall in the identity God gave you. You are not what others whispered, not what your circumstances suggested, not even what your fears tried to convince you of. You are more than enough, because you are exactly who God says you are.

Walk boldly now. Walk as one who knows that your current condition does not diminish your calling, that your strength does not depend on their approval, that your value is not up for debate. You don't have to prove a thing, not to them, not to yourself, not even to the enemy.

You've been formed with intention, called with purpose, and covered with grace. So live like it. Breathe like it. Love like it. Leave here today secure enough to declare:

"I am who God says I am, and that is enough."

EPILOGUE

KEEP LOOKING IN THE MIRROR, UNTIL YOU DON'T SEE THE PROBLEM ANYMORE

You made it.

You've stared into the mirror of God's Word. You've faced down every flaw you thought disqualified you. You've wrestled with your fears, your failures, and your false identities. You've done the mirror work, and you're still standing.

But here's the beautiful truth: if you keep looking in the mirror long enough, you'll stop seeing the problem and start seeing the promise.

You'll stop seeing all the ways you think you've fallen short and start seeing the ways God has carried you through.

You'll stop obsessing over your scars and start recognizing them as the evidence of your survival.

You'll stop comparing yourself to others and start standing in the fullness of who God made you to be.

That's wholeness.

Wholeness is when your reflection no longer reminds you of what you've lost but reveals what you've gained.

Wholeness is when you stop begging for permission to exist and start walking confidently in your divine assignment.

Wholeness is when the whispers of the enemy no longer drown out the Word of your Father.

Wholeness is when you no longer measure yourself by your wounds but by His work.

So what does a whole and healed man look like?

A whole man stands tall, not because he's never been knocked down, but because he knows who picked him back up.

He wears his scars like medals, not shackles.

He speaks with clarity, not to convince others of his worth but to carry truth wherever he goes.

He walks into rooms without shrinking, because he's not intimidated by the opinions of others.

He can lead with humility, love with vulnerability, and worship with abandon.

His presence brings peace, not pressure.

He listens more than he defends, gives more than he grasps, blesses more than he battles.

A whole and healed man is not perfect, but he is free.

Free from the need to perform.

Free from the fear of failure.

Free from the weight of comparison.

Free to show up fully, as himself, in every space God has assigned him to.

When I look in the mirror now, I see a man who has nothing left to prove, yet everything left to give.

I see a man who no longer hides his hurt or hustles for validation.

I see a man who can love himself and others without condition because he finally believes what his Father said about him from the start.

I see a man who has traded striving for stillness, and shame for sonship.

That's who I am.

And that's who you are becoming.

So keep looking in the mirror.

Until what you see aligns with what God said.

Until your reflection no longer condemns you but confirms you.

Until you realize the man in the mirror isn't a problem to fix, he's a testimony of grace.

You have nothing left to prove.

Just more to reflect.

More to reveal.

More to become.

Look again.

And when you look this time... see the whole and healed man God created you to be.

You are exactly who He says you are, and that's more than enough.

NAPOLEON'S EPILOGUE
THE MAN IN THE MIRROR, TODAY

The boy in the introduction was broken.

The man writing these words is whole.

Not perfect, but whole.

Not without scars, but healed enough to stand in them and still smile.

Not free from memory, but free from shame.

When I look in the mirror today, I don't just see my reflection, I see redemption.

I see the man God always knew I could become, even when I didn't believe it myself.

I see a husband who has learned to show up fully present, to love with honesty, to listen more than defend, to lead with tenderness.

I see a father who honors the memory of his children and cherishes the ones entrusted to his care.

I see a son who no longer hides behind performance but rests in the knowledge that he is already enough.

I see a preacher who doesn't just deliver sermons but embodies them, who ministers from a place of healed wounds, not hidden ones.

I see a Black man who has reclaimed his dignity, his voice, and his value, not based on titles, applause, or possessions, but rooted in the unshakable truth of who God says he is.

I see a leader who has learned that strength is not about how loud you roar but how deeply you love and how faithfully you serve.

The man I am today has nothing left to prove.

I no longer chase affirmation because I already have it.

I no longer sabotage my own peace to please others.

I no longer let my past disqualify my future.

I still go to therapy, not because I'm broken beyond repair but because healing is not a destination, it's a discipline.

I still lean on brothers, not because I'm weak but because wholeness is communal, not individual.

I still wake up some mornings with whispers of doubt, but now I know how to silence them with the Word.

The man in the mirror is no longer defined by his mistakes.

The man in the mirror is no longer ashamed of his scars.

The man in the mirror has learned to love himself, because he finally believes what his Father said all along:

"You are my son. In you, I am well pleased."

To the boy I was, thank you for surviving long enough to become the man I am.

To the man I am, thank you for doing the work to become whole.

And to the man I'm still becoming, keep looking in the mirror.

Because even now, God is not finished.

This is what wholeness looks like today.

And if He could do it for me, He can do it for you too.

So look again.

And when you do, see the whole, healed man God created you to be.

Because you are exactly who He says you are, and that is more than enough.

ABOUT THE AUTHOR

Napoleon Bradford

Napoleon Abram Bradford, D.Min. Ed.S, a native of Sumter, SC, residing in Bowie, MD., is a distinguished leader in spiritual and community engagement. He is a devoted family man — a son, sibling, husband, father, and grandfather — whose life reflects a commitment to service across multiple arenas.

Napoleon currently serves as the first-ever Chaplain for the Defense Counterintelligence and Security Agency (DCSA) in Quantico, VA, and Ft. Meade, MD, a national position in the U.S. Federal Government. He is also a Brigade Chaplain (Captain) for the 59th Troop Command in the South Carolina Army National Guard, providing spiritual guidance and support to military personnel. In addition, he is the CEO and Principal Counselor Consultant at

The Place Center for Healing and Wholeness, a counseling and personal development institution he founded.

As the convener of the **Cathedral of Champions**, Napoleon is a sought-after public speaker, presenting at national conferences on intergenerational trauma, self-sabotage, and the critical role of paternal participation in pregnancy. His insights into these issues have earned him recognition as a thought leader in faith-based and therapeutic communities.

Napoleon is a prolific author, contributing to both books and academic journals. His works include **Daily L.I.F.E. Volumes 1 & 2: Lessons for Living in Faith Every Day**, the recently published **Strength from My Storms: Lessons I Learned Going Through**, and **Let "IT" Go: A Lenten-Style Devotion for Releasing Negativity**.

His academic journey reflects a profound dedication to learning and spiritual leadership. Napoleon holds a Bachelor of Science in Elementary Education from Morris College, a Master's in School Counseling, and a Specialist in School Administration from Bowling Green State University. He earned a Master of Divinity from the Samuel DeWitt Proctor School of Theology at Virginia Union University and two Doctor of Ministry degrees from the Virginia University of Lynchburg and Virginia Union University, respectively. Currently, he is pursuing a Ph.D. in Public Theology and Community Engagement at Hampton University.

Napoleon is married to **Dr. Karen Stacey Hilton Bradford**, his first-grade crush and life partner. Together, they co-founded **The Perfecting PLACE**, an interactive faith community centered on welcoming and uplifting people seeking personal growth, healing, and spiritual connection.

www.ingramcontent.com/pod-product-compliance
Lightning Source LLC
Chambersburg PA
CBHW051139120626
46547CB00012B/868